THE BARBARA KRAUS
INTERNATIONAL COOKBOOK

Other Books by Barbara Kraus

The Dictionary of Sodium, Fats, and Cholesterol
The Barbara Kraus Calorie Counter
The Barbara Kraus Cholesterol Counter
The Barbara Kraus 30-Day Cholesterol Program
Calories & Carbohydrates
Barbara Kraus Calorie Guide
Barbara Kraus Carbohydrate Guide
Barbara Kraus Complete Guide to Sodium
Barbara Kraus Sodium Guide to Brand Names & Basic Foods

THE BARBARA KRAUS INTERNATIONAL COOKBOOK

ADAPTED AND EDITED BY
MARGARET MARKHAM

A PERIGEE BOOK

*For Leslie Markham and Anne Ternes,
and a healthier life for future generations*

Perigee Books
are published by
The Putnam Publishing Group
200 Madison Avenue
New York, NY 10016

Copyright © 1991 by Margaret Markham and Margaret Ternes
All rights reserved. This book, or parts thereof, may not be reproduced in
any form without permission.
Published simultaneously in Canada

Library of Congress Cataloging-in-Publication Data

Kraus, Barbara.
The Barbara Kraus international cookbook/adapted and edited by
Margaret Markham.
p.   cm.
"A Perigee book."
Includes indexes.
ISBN 0-399-51655-7
1. Cookery, International.   I. Markham, Margaret.   II. Title.
TX725.A1K688   1991   90-32448 CIP
641.59—dc20

Cover design copyright © 1991 by Mike McIver
Printed in the United States of America
1 2 3 4 5 6 7 8 9 10

CONTENTS

FOREWORD

Anyone who ever had the pleasure of joining Barbara Kraus at a meal prepared by her knows that to her, cooking was never a chore, but a challenge. By her standard, even the simplest dishes deserve a touch of glamour. To achieve that end, Barbara collected tantalizing recipes from outstanding American restaurants, 150 of which were represented in one of her works, *The Cookbook to Serve 2, 6 or 24*.

But Barbara's interests ranged far beyond the boundaries of her own country. Inspired by her background in anthropology, she was inevitably led to cull recipes from all over the world. Some 350 of them appeared in her epic collection, *The Cookbook of the United Nations*.

At the same time, keenly aware that the food we choose has a direct impact on well-being, Barbara became one of the pioneers in reshaping American eating habits with her bestseller, *Calories and Carbohydrates*. This was soon followed by the ground-breaking *Dictionary of Sodium, Fats, and Cholesterol*. For nigh on two decades, her books have awakened millions of readers to nutrition-consciousness and helped alert them to the importance of counting calories and reading labels.

This new international cookbook combines two of Barbara's main goals—glamorizing everyday meals with unusual, intriguing dishes from far-off places, and cooking more health-consciously. To that end we have re-created some of her favorite recipes but with reduced levels of cholesterol, fat, or sodium, all of which many Americans are now anxious to minimize.

In no sense is this book meant to serve as the sole basis for a strict diet regimen. For that it is best to consult your doctor. Rather, we hope to encourage readers to discover for themselves that food with less cholesterol, fat, or sodium can be satisfying and delectable. We hope that once you've tried some of these recipes, you'll agree that healthier eating does not mean an automatic sentence to uninteresting, tasteless meals. In Barbara's own words: These dishes really are fun to cook and deliciously different to taste. *Bon appetit* and exciting "exploration" in your own kitchen.

—Margaret Markham

PREFACE

Background

In the last couple of decades, American eating patterns have been changing slowly but quite dramatically. More and more people have come to realize that slim is better than considerably overweight. Thus, the emphasis now is on fewer calories, and for the sake of better health, on less fat, cholesterol, and sodium.

The American Heart Association, along with other major medical organizations, has urged the general public to consume a diet with no more than 30 percent of the total calories in the form of fat, 55 percent as carbohydrates, and 15 as protein. The cholesterol intake for the average person should be limited to less than 300 milligrams per day.

There is a wide variety of culinary choices for curbing the intake of cholesterol, fats, and sodium. The recipes in this book have been selected precisely for that purpose. We have chosen these international recipes in the hope they will provide a touch of glamour and impart new zest to your everyday dining, as well as to festive occasions—yet without the penalty of an overabundance of cholesterol, fats, or sodium.

Also, many of the individual dishes in this volume can be incorporated into a medically supervised regimen by determining the exact amount of specific nutrients in any recipe, and then checking with your doctor or nutrition counselor to make doubly sure your choices are acceptable. Resources you can consult for precise information are, for example, *The Barbara Kraus Cholesterol Counter*, and the *Complete Guide to Sodium*. They list the amount of particular elements in thousands of food items, generally by brand name and household measure.

There are other easy steps you can take in preparing meals at home to help lower your family's intake of cholesterol, fats, and salt. These are given in "Hints for Healthier Cooking," starting on page 11.

Format

To help you enjoy preparing the dishes in this book, we've included some special features we hope you'll find both useful and efficient.

The "Seasoning Guide" (see page 15) lists many commonly available seasonings and the dishes in which they are most frequently used.

To make it easier to explore dishes from many lands, we've given the country or region of origin at the top of each recipe along with its name. A special index at the back lists recipes by country or region. Are you in the mood for dining in tropical Africa near a glistening ocean, but you can't leave home? Just turn to that index, find the page for the Ivory Coast, and savor Chicken with Peanut Butter Sauce.

At the top of each recipe entry, below the name, is the yield or number of suggested servings. Keep in mind, of course, that such estimations are general. Serving sizes vary according to custom, taste, appetite, and special diet requirements.

The approximate time needed to make the dish is also given near the top of the recipe to help you plan your cooking schedule more quickly and accurately. Remember that this, too, is a generalization.

Similarly, the listings of ingredients and equipment are designed to avoid the annoying experience we've all had, probably more than once—the sudden, frustrating discovery that the dish you're in the midst of preparing requires a cooking utensil you don't have, or an ingredient you overlooked in your first quick reading. This should prove helpful in advance, both in planning your marketing list and in getting everything lined up on your work surface, ready for you to begin cooking.

Finally, to make it easier to grasp in a single reading exactly what you need to do in each recipe, we've separated the mechanics of the process by listing the steps. To make Albanian Chicken with Walnut Sauce, for example, you can tell at a quick glance you'll have to preheat the oven, take out a blender, food processor, or rolling pin to crush the nuts, and plan your mealtime to let the finished dish "stand" for up to ten minutes before serving. In this way, once you're ready to roll up your sleeves and start cooking, you can do it more efficiently and more smoothly in assembly-line fashion.

HINTS FOR HEALTHIER COOKING

It's not as hard as many people think to take the first steps toward healthier cooking and healthier eating. It's a good idea to start with four simple rules:

1. Reading labels and checking ingredients are musts.
2. Moderation is the motto when it comes to portion size or to the amount of added ingredients that may be medically questionable.
3. Meals should be planned ahead as much as possible to balance the overall intake of the essential nutrients in the course of the week, rather than for only one day now and then.
4. Cooking practices usually need to be modified to reduce intake of unwanted calories, cholesterol, fats, or sodium.

Reading Labels

Fortunately for consumers, a great many food companies have responded to the public's need and desire to know exactly how much they are consuming in terms of calories or any given ingredient in processed foods. Label information becomes an integral part of healthier eating and better menu planning. *Read the entire label* and remember that the item listed first is the one present in highest volume.

Although some companies have made the job easier for us by listing ingredients, as yet not all food companies are required to show these precise amounts. This means that in addition to checking labels, you are likely to need a second reference source to complete the food-intake profile, especially when shopping for fresh foods. One such work is *The Dictionary of Sodium, Fats, and Cholesterol* by Barbara Kraus. Publications of this type will help you, for example, to find out not only how much sodium there is in a fresh cucumber, but also to compare how much is added in some of the most common brands of various types of pickles.

Moderation

More and more people are being advised by their doctors to watch how much they eat and what kinds of foods they select. Moderation in the number of calories we eat and in the food constituents we take in can help keep us on the right track for better health, now and in the years ahead. It's usually easier to learn to limit portion size and reduce the extra salt or butter in cooking gradually, than to do it all in one fell swoop. That applies not only to what is added during cooking but also to what is added at the table, whether it be butter, salt, salad dressing, or other sources of cholesterol, fats, or sodium.

Balance

In planning menus, nutritionists have long advocated choosing a wide variety of foods as the basis of healthy eating. In general that still holds true. But it's not the whole story. It's also important to choose foods that will give you the best nutritive values without adding too many unwanted calories or too much cholesterol, fat, or sodium. This is a process of self-education that takes time. You need to learn to plan ahead to check the week's nutrition score, rather than picking just any recipe on the impulse of the moment. The payoff is in healthier cooking and wiser eating habits.

With the exception of those on a highly restricted, medically supervised diet, the vast majority of people have a wider choice of food than ever before in history. That also holds true in selecting recipes that will add variety to a balanced diet.

Cooking Practices

Modifying cooking habits can be a surprisingly big step toward healthier meals. That goes for both the selection of food items and the way they are prepared.

Here are some practical tips:

Frying. If you choose to use this cooking method, try polyunsaturated cooking oil; there are now many brands available in the supermarkets. Make sure the frying temperature is high enough so the outside of the food cooks quickly and soaks up the least possible amount of fat. As an alternate to frying breaded chicken or vegetables in the traditional deep-fat way, oven bake them in a pan with nonstick surface.

Roasting. A rack beneath the meat or fowl will help drain off the surplus fat that seeps from the tissues under high heat. If basting is necessary to keep the roast from drying out, don't use the drippings; try a polyunsaturated vegetable oil instead, or use broth skimmed of fat.

Grilling/Broiling. Use a rack, for the same reason as for roasting.

Wok cooking. This method has become popular, and for good reason. Minimum oil is required for very hot, very fast cooking. Many wok recipes also emphasize using strips of lean meat along with a large proportion of fresh vegetables. This automatically reduces the total amount of beef, pork, or lamb in each portion served.

Trimming. Eliminating visible fat, even with leaner cuts, or completely removing chicken skin is a big plus. Trimming won't eliminate cholesterol inherent in meat or poultry tissues, but it will help reduce the amount of saturated fat, and the total fat, on your table.

Skimming. Removing fat from soups, stews, pot roasts, and gravies is a simple and obvious but often overlooked way of cutting down the amount of fat in final servings. Whenever possible, prepare such dishes with enough standing time to let the fat rise to the top, either at room temperature or in the refrigerator. The fat will form a layer, or "cake," which can be easily removed.

Selecting. Choosing foods clearly labeled as low, reduced, or free of any unwanted ingredients can help keep the nutrition score within desirable limits.

Desserts. Sweets need not be given up entirely. Look for fruit compotes or puddings, or cakes made with egg whites instead of whole eggs. If you can't give up your favorite cake recipe that calls for whole eggs, use an egg substitute or double up on the amount of egg whites used and cut down to at least half the yolks.

Chocolate. This universal favorite may still be used in recipes for special occasions. To cut down on saturated fat, try using cocoa and oil (3 tablespoons cocoa plus 1 tablespoon polyunsaturated oil) for each 1-ounce square of chocolate called for.

Milk. In puddings, soups, and baked items, whole milk can often be replaced by skim or low-fat.

Cream. Many dishes call for cream in some form—ice cream, whipped cream, sour cream, and so on. Instead, use low-fat or nonfat yogurt routinely in your cooking. In place of the sour cream in various dishes, dips, and sauces, substitute low-fat plain yogurt or blenderized low-fat cottage cheese.

Butter. Like lard and other saturated fats, this can be replaced by a carefully chosen vegetable oil or margarine. Check the label to see if you're getting the kind of fat best suited for your nutritional needs. For making cakes, cookies, and desserts, switch to polyunsaturated fats whenever possible; with these the amount of fat can be reduced usually by one-fourth to one-third.

Toppings. Real whipped cream and other additions are hard to resist on desserts. But ice-cold evaporated skim milk can be whipped to a delicious topping that doesn't arouse feelings of guilt.

Salad dressing. This is almost an everyday item on many family tables. In place of the usually rich mayonnaise or prepared salad dressings, try blenderized low-fat cottage cheese, yogurt, or polyunsaturated vegetable oils; lemon juice or vinegar; and herbs and spices in your own customized version.

Stuffing. Stuffing is a favorite side dish in many countries. It soaks up all the juices inside or under the skin of the bird or meat during roasting. Unfortunately, an appreciable part of the juices absorbed by the stuffing consists of fatty substances, including cholesterol. For that reason, if you have to keep close tabs on intake of cholesterol and fats, it's better to add a minimal amount of desired fat or oil to the stuffing and bake it in a separate pan or cook it on the stove.

At first, modifying cooking habits may seem intimidating. But if you approach it in a spirit of culinary adventure and realize it calls for a little trial and error, you'll soon find the outcome rewarding, both in health and in enjoyment of pleasing new dishes.

SEASONING GUIDE

Somehow, it seems the things we should give up are usually the most desirable and delectable. There's an obvious reason why certain staples, such as butter, lard, bacon or chicken fat, fat-laden goose liver, and salt, have been used internationally for countless generations. They impart a wonderful flavor and aroma and add zest to our dishes. But there's a simple way to overcome these tempting items. When cooking, experiment with the wide array of herbs, spices, and other seasonings available at your grocery. They will introduce your taste buds to new sensations and bring fresh excitement to your cooking. If you're using a seasoning for the first time, however, be cautious. Try just a little to see whether you like it. You can always add more, but you can't take it out if you've hastily put in too much. Below, for easy reference, we've listed forty-four seasonings commonly available, along with suggestions for their use.

Allspice   A spicy but mild, slightly sweet blend of cinnamon, nutmeg, and cloves. Often used in cakes, cookies, and dried or stewed fruits, and with cranberries. Adds a pungent touch to baked ham and broiled steak.

Anise   Licorice-like flavor and aroma. Used in rolls, cookies, coffee cakes, pie fillings, and sweet pickles. Small amount (chopped) imparts delicate flavor to salads.

Basil   Widely used in Italian cooking, especially in pasta dishes and with tomato sauces, as well as in salads. Adds rich, pungent note to meat, poultry, and seafood stews.

Bay leaves   Mild flavor, but too much can give a bitter taste. Excellent in pot roasts and with braised or roast chicken.

Borage   Crisp, cucumberlike flavor. Can be used raw, steamed, or sautéed, or as garnish. Leaves and stems enhance flavor of many vegetables and green salads, as well as fish and poultry dishes. Often added to beverages, pickles, sauces, and salad dressings.

Bouquet garni   Ready-to-use mixture of seasonings (celery, parsley, basil, savory, marjoram, onion, bay leaf, thyme) tied together in a "bouquet" and wrapped in a cloth bag or cheesecloth. Gives particularly rich, savory flavor to slow-cooking dishes such as potted chuck steak and bean dishes.

Caraway   Mild flavor. Available fresh, chopped, or dried, and used in breads, rolls, roasts, and dips.

Caraway seeds   May be used in place of fresh herb. Often added to rye bread for zesty taste. Gives unusual touch to cole slaw and many other cabbage dishes.

Cardamom   Slightly bittersweet. Widely mixed in or sprinkled on top of coffee cakes and pastries. Gives rich taste to sweet potato and pumpkin dishes.

Cayenne   Sharp, hot-tasting powdered red pepper that livens fish dishes, grilled or stewed meats, and bland vegetables. Often used in deviled eggs and atop baked potatoes.

Celery seeds   Celerylike flavor, but slightly on the bitter side. Most commonly used in chowders, fish dishes, meat loaf, salad dressings, and stewed vegetables (tomatoes, cabbage, okra).

Chervil   Flavor somewhat similar to parsley or tarragon. Gives particularly intriguing results when used with basil or chives. Enhances flavor in salads and chicken and fish dishes.

Chili powder   May be pure ground chili pepper, but may also be a blend with oregano, cumin, garlic, and salt. Often very "hot." Distinctive flavor is used to enliven Mexican dishes; a favorite in chili con carne and seasoned rice or meat dishes.

Chives   Delicate onionlike flavor perks up taste when chopped and added to salads or dips.

Cilantro   Also known as coriander. Has rather sagelike flavor. Adds sharp taste to many foods, including potatoes, beets, and onions. Also used in clam and oyster dishes.

Cinnamon   Widely used in cakes, spice cookies, and sweet potato and pumpkin dishes. A delightful surprise with squash or peas. Traditionally added to coffee or mulled cider in some countries.

Cloves   Pungent, spicy, but sweetish. Wide array of uses: in pies, baked beans, creamed vegetable soups, tomato aspic, chicken and pork dishes, and stewed fruits, among others. Frequently combined with lemon or orange rind in spicy teas.

Cumin   Tangy flavor that lends zest to chili, stews, rice, and fish dishes. Often used in Mexican dishes.

Curry   Usually hot seasoning, but may be mild. Imparts exotic
powder   flavor and golden color. Livens taste in soups and fish and poultry dishes. May be sprinkled on nuts for a snack. Widely used in Oriental and Middle Eastern recipes.

Dill   Delicate but piquant flavor. Widely used in pickling. Livens up salads, soups (when chopped and sprinkled on hot or cold creamed soups), potato dishes (such as potato salad), eggs, and vegetables.

Fennel   Similar to the licorice-like flavor of anise. Fresh leaves excellent in salads or as lacelike garnish. Suitable in a variety of dishes, including breads and fish, fowl, egg, rice, lentil, and cabbage recipes.

Garlic   Especially when fresh, has a nippy taste that puts a mild "bite" in stews, braised meats, roasts, salad dressings, and bland vegetables.

Ginger   Used in many typically Oriental dishes, squash dishes, and pumpkin pie, and along with other spices in cakes, cookies, and stewed fruits.

Grenadine   Thick, sweet red pomegranate syrup. Adds color to fruits, ices, sauces, puddings, and drinks.

Mace   Similar to nutmeg flavor. Adds exotic touch to fruit pies, stews, fish dishes, pickled foods, and cakes, including gingerbread.

Marjoram   Slightly pungent yet delicate. Brings to life the flavor in poultry, chops, roasts, and stews.

Mint   Uniquely aromatic flavor and scent, prized since ancient times. Used in a wide array of foods and beverages, including fruit salads and tea, and a favorite seasoning for lamb and veal.

Mustard   Zesty taste ranges from mild to very sharp. Used in "hot" Oriental sauces, vegetables, ground meats, salad dressings, poultry, and creamed dishes.

Nutmeg   A must in eggnog, custards, and puddings. Adds a tangy touch to coffee cakes, pumpkin or sweet potato pie, spice cake, and cookies.

Oregano   Rather peppery flavor makes it an indispensable ingredient in many sauces and meat dishes, especially for Italian cuisine. Adds gusto to pizza and hearty soups such as minestrone and pepper pot, to shellfish dishes, and to bland vegetables.

Paprika   Lends both color and mild flavor to many dishes. Sweet Hungarian variety is basic ingredient in goulash and paprikas made with meat or poultry. Often sprinkled on canapés, creamed soups, chowders, and casseroles to add a bright touch.

Parsley   Available fresh, chopped, or dried, and commonly used in soups, salads, potato dishes, and stews. Often appears as a fresh decorative touch on salads.

Pepper   Both black and white varieties give a lingering "bite" to many dishes. Best when freshly ground. White variety is preferred when flecks of black would mar appearance of the food.

Poppy   Tiny, crisp, crunchy, somewhat nutty-tasting. Add flavor and provide decoration on top of breads, cakes, and rolls.
seeds

Rosemary   Pungent aroma and flavor when used fresh, but more delicate in dried form. Used internationally in many meat and poultry dishes. Helps in fully blending the flavors of other seasonings in meat dishes, especially roasts and barbecues.

Saffron   Widely treasured for its unique, captivating flavor and for the reddish-orange color it imparts, especially to white rice. A major ingredient in Spanish cooking.

Sage   Somewhat bitter, often lemony flavor. Adds a popular note to many meats, such as veal, lamb, and poultry. Fresh young leaves can also be added to salads. Perks up bland- or mild-tasting vegetables such as squash, artichokes, lentils, and potatoes.

Savory   Mild, tangy taste. Often added to poultry stuffing, meat loaf, salads, and egg dishes. Also used in teas, soups, and many vegetable dishes, including those made with snap beans, eggplant, asparagus, Brussels sprouts.

Scallion   Mildly onion-flavored vegetable. Used in either raw or cooked dishes, stews, casseroles, and sauces. Highly desirable when the stronger flavor and aroma of onions are to be avoided. Chopped green stalks add color and zest to fresh salads.

Sesame seeds	Provide crunchy texture in salad dressings and atop salads, and when sprinkled on cookies, rolls, or bread.
Shallot	Delicate flavor reminiscent of both garlic and onion, and excellent substitute when those stronger flavors are undesirable. Highly prized in French dishes.
Tarragon	Piquant flavor makes it ideal in marinades, soups, and egg dishes and with bland vegetables.
Thyme	Delicate yet slightly pungent flavor and aroma. A requisite in seasoning mixtures such as bouquet garni, and a favorite in tomato sauces and stewed tomatoes, meat and poultry dishes, hearty fish soups and stews, and with cooked and raw vegetables, such as spinach, cucumbers, mushrooms, and peas.
Turmeric	Reminiscent of saffron but somewhat more bitter. Can be used as a less costly substitute for saffron. Common in rice dishes, seafood recipes such as chowders, braised or roast meats, and pickled dishes.

ABBREVIATIONS, SYMBOLS, EQUIVALENTS, AND ALTITUDE ADJUSTMENTS

Abbreviations

Tb(s) = Tablespoon(s)
tsp(s) = teaspoon(s)
oz(s) = ounce(s)
pt(s) = pint(s)
qt(s) = quart(s)
lb(s) = pound(s)
fl = fluid
& = and
canned = in bottles, jars, or cans

Weight

1 pound = 16 ounces
1 ounce = 28.35 grams
3.52 ounces = 100 grams

Volume

1 quart = 32 fluid ounces
1 cup = 8 fluid ounces
1 cup = ½ pint
1 cup = 16 tablespoons
1 fluid ounce = 2 tablespoons

Some Useful Equivalents

1 tablespoon = 3 teaspoons
2 tablespoons = ⅛ cup
5 tablespoons plus 1 teaspoon = ⅓ cup
8–10 egg whites = 1 cup
1 lemon = 3 tablespoons juice*
1 orange = ⅓ cup juice*
4 slices bread = 1 cup dry crumbs*
14 graham crackers = 1 cup finely crushed

*Average values

1 medium banana = ⅓ cup mashed
1 medium peach or pear = ½ cup sliced
1 small pressed garlic clove = ⅛ teaspoon garlic powder
1 pound dry beans = 6 cups cooked
1 pound carrots = 2½ cups chopped
1 large green pepper = 1 cup chopped
8 ounces spaghetti (uncooked) = 4 cups cooked
1 cup long-grain rice (uncooked) = 3 cups cooked
8-ounce can = 1 cup*
1 no. 2 can = 2½ cups*
1 no. 3 can = 4 cups*

Ingredient Substitutes

1 ounce chocolate = 3–4 tablespoons cocoa + ½ tablespoon solid fat
1 tablespoon prepared mustard = 1 teaspoon dry mustard
1 cup whole milk = ½ cup evaporated milk + ½ cup water, or 1 cup reconstituted nonfat dry milk + 1 tablespoon butter
1 cup sour milk = 1 cup milk + 1 tablespoon vinegar or lemon juice, stirred

General Scale of Oven Temperatures

450–500°F = very hot
400–450° = hot
375–400° = medium hot
325–375° = moderate
300–325° = slow
250–300° = very slow
200–250° = keeps food warm

Adjustments for High Altitude

Unlike physics or chemistry, cooking is not an exact science with predictably uniform results throughout the world. There is no absolute guarantee that the same recipe will always give identical results, even in the same kitchen: atmospheric conditions, different equipment, and a different cook can all influence the outcome.

*Average values

If a recipe does not come out as expected the first time, don't be discouraged. Try making some adjustment to meet your particular needs.

The following table gives a few examples of changes that are usually necessary at the given altitudes above sea level:

INGREDIENT	CHANGE AT 3,000 FEET	CHANGE AT 5,000 FEET
Baking powder for each teaspoon	Reduce by $\frac{1}{8}$ teaspoon	Reduce by $\frac{1}{8}$–$\frac{1}{4}$ teaspoon
Sugar for each cup	Reduce by up to 1 tablespoon	Reduce by up to 2 tablespoons
Liquid for each cup	Add 1–2 tablespoons	Add 3–4 tablespoons
Flour for each cup	Add 1 tablespoon	Add 1–2 tablespoons
Oven temperature	No change	Add 25°F
Simmering or braising meats	No change	Add 25 percent more time

PART I
Reduced Cholesterol Recipes

INTRODUCTION

The role of cholesterol is actually a Jekyll-and-Hyde story—both good and bad. Cholesterol is one of the essential substances in human physiology and metabolism. A considerable amount of cholesterol is produced in our bodies, in addition to what we get in our meals and between-meal snacks. Too little cholesterol can retard health and normal development. Too much can endanger life.

Cholesterol is involved in many of the body's vital biochemical cycles, for instance, the production of certain vitamins and steroid hormones, including sex hormones. It is also necessary for forming bile in the liver. Without bile, fatty foods cannot be readily digested and absorbed. That's part of the good side.

What about the bad side? Excessive cholesterol in the blood contributes to the development of atherosclerotic plaques. These formations clog arterial passages and obstruct blood flow, often leading to painful angina and to heart attacks. In other parts of the body, cholesterol deposits that impede circulation through an artery can also trigger devastating effects. Blocking blood flow in the brain can induce hemorrhaging or even a stroke. Sluggish circulation in the legs can produce disabling muscle cramps or encourage infection, sometimes to the point of gangrene.

In addition to the good and bad types of cholesterol, we also need to keep an eye on the level of triglycerides, substances derived from fats and oils. These compounds have often been found in high concentration in the bloodstream of patients who suffered heart attacks or strokes. If we customarily eat too much animal fat or even vegetable oils, we are likely to have too many triglycerides released into the bloodstream. Much of it ends up stored in cells as fat.

According to a study recently reported in the *Journal of the American Medical Association*, about 60 million Americans aged twenty or more already face the risk of coronary heart disease because of their blood cholesterol levels. Coronary disease is now listed by the National Center for Health Statistics as the nation's number-one killer.

A statement from the American Medical Association underscores that same point: More than half of all adults in the United States have blood cholesterol levels that place them at an increased risk for coronary heart disease. Even more significant, about 50 percent of this group have values over 240 milligrams per deciliter, a level that more than doubles their risk of heart attacks. Nevertheless, according to medical experts, most such adults can reduce their cholesterol levels into the desirable range (under 200 mg/dl) through diet and exercise.

As scientists delve more deeply into how our bodies make and handle cholesterol, it's increasingly clear that it is not a simple process. Our metabolism produces various forms of fatty molecules. Crucial to the cholesterol story are substances known as lipoproteins. These are packets of fat and cholesterol that ride piggyback on protein molecules which carry them in the bloodstream. One such complex, known as "bad cholesterol," is low-density lipoprotein (LDL). The other, dubbed "good cholesterol," is high-density lipoprotein (HDL). When you have too much of the LDL circulating in your body, it may get dumped onto arterial walls.

HDL behaves quite differently. It can snatch the cholesterol deposits off arterial walls. Obviously, if we can keep the level of bad cholesterol to a minimum and increase the level of good cholesterol, we encourage our system to scour the cholesterol off arterial walls by a perfectly natural procedure.

Some of the latest studies suggest that there may be yet another way of deterring formation of plaque. According to Dr. Hermann Esterbauer of the University of Graz, in Austria, the "bad" cholesterol, which sets the stage for later heart attacks, becomes a threat only after it undergoes a chemical change known as oxidation. Apparently, LDL normally travels in the company of a number of natural substances that prevent oxidation, including the familiar nutrients vitamin E and beta carotene.

When stripped of such protection, LDL rapidly oxidizes. Several scientists now propose that oxidized LDL is especially appetizing to scavenger cells, known as macrophages, which literally gobble it up. When macrophages become bloated with oxidized LDL, they form clusters just inside the walls of blood vessels. This, a number of researchers believe, is the first step in the formation of plaque.

Encouraged by such evidence, researchers at the Pasteur Institute in France have launched clinical studies to monitor the effect of antioxidant therapy in patients with high cholesterol levels. Their preliminary findings indicate that when protective substances, for instance vitamin E, are given along with a cholesterol-lowering drug, cholesterol levels may be lowered and the risk of heart attack reduced.

Many individuals can avoid excessively high cholesterol by cutting down on foods high in cholesterol and saturated fats and emphasizing those that may help clear the body of the bad cholesterol. Oat bran, green beans, and other foods with appreciable amounts of fiber may help reduce serum cholesterol levels.

In an evaluation of this dietary trend, the Council on Scientific Affairs of the American Medical Association confirmed in its own journal in mid-1989 that the natural fibers in fresh fruits, vegetables, legumes, oat bran, and barley appear to have the most potential for reducing cholesterol levels.

But that's by no means the complete solution to the problem, Purdue University physiologist Jon A. Story reported at a recent meeting of the American Chemical Society. Bile acids, of which we have five distinct types derived from cholesterol, also play key roles in cholesterol reduction, Story says. "The findings reinforce what we already know about nutrition—that a balanced diet, rather than a cure-all such as oat bran, still is the answer."

Foods of animal origin, such as fish and shellfish, meat, milk, and cheese, do contain cholesterol. Plants, on the other hand, do not synthesize cholesterol. Hence, fruits and vegetables, nuts and grains do not add to our cholesterol burden. On the other hand, there are many foods, including a few vegetables, that contain fats or oils of the undesirable, saturated type. This is the kind that prompts your liver to produce more cholesterol (see the introduction to Part II).

Cooking fats to be avoided in particular are those that solidify at room temperature, such as lard, butter, and coconut oil, as well as suet and rendered bacon or poultry fat. Whole-milk and whole-egg solids and chocolate likewise contain saturated fats. Vegetable oils high in saturated fat to be avoided or used only very sparingly include coconut, palm-kernel, and palm oils.

As noted in the foreword, this collection of recipes is not intended as the sole basis for a highly restricted medical diet and should not be used for that purpose unless so approved by your doctor. However, many dishes in the following section contain less cholesterol than traditional recipes and are suitable for inclusion in less restricted diets. We offer them in the hope of encouraging you to plan interesting and unusual menus that will not add excessive amounts of cholesterol to your meals and will help keep your family's blood cholesterol levels in the healthy range.

CHINA **STUFFED TOMATOES**

SERVINGS: 8

TIME NEEDED: 40 minutes, plus soaking and steaming time

INGREDIENTS

1 large dried Chinese
  mushroom
1½ cups water
8 small slicing tomatoes
½ cup minced cooked chicken
½ cup minced, very lean,
  trimmed cooked ham

¼ cup chopped cooked fish
  fillet (cod, halibut, haddock,
  or perch)
1 garlic clove, minced
½ tsp minced fresh ginger
1 Tb margarine

EQUIPMENT

medium bowl   medium saucepan   chopper   vegetable steamer or
colander in 7-qt Dutch oven

PREPARATION

Soak   mushroom in bowl with ½ cup water for 15 minutes; then
drain.

Heat   1 cup water in saucepan to boiling, and dip tomatoes
briefly into it to remove skins.

Cut   tops off tomatoes, thickly enough to keep them as "caps";
then scoop out center of each tomato.

Mince   mushroom (discard stem) and return it to bowl.

Add   chicken, ham, fish, garlic, and ginger to mushroom.

Melt   margarine and add it to mushroom mixture, blending well.

Fill   tomato shells with mushroom mixture and replace tops
firmly.

Arrange   stuffed tomatoes in top of steamer with 2 inches of water
at the bottom.

Heat   to boiling over moderate heat and steam, covered, 15 minutes.

If any stuffing is left over, it can be added to a Cauliflower-Cucumber
Sauce (page 52), which is poured hot over the tomato appetizer or
served on the side.

CZECHOSLOVAKIA   HAM AND APPLE
ROLLS

YIELD: 16 rolls
TIME NEEDED: 30 minutes

INGREDIENTS

2 Tbs prepared horseradish   ⅛ tsp white pepper
2 Tbs yogurt   1 large apple, peeled
3½ tsps lemon juice   8 thin slices lean boiled ham

EQUIPMENT

2 small bowls   toothpicks

PREPARATION

Blend   horseradish, yogurt, ½ tsp lemon juice, and white pepper in
        bowl.
Cut   apple into 8 thin slices; then divide each slice in half.
Dip   apple slices into remaining lemon juice in bowl.
Cut   ham slices in half.
Put   ½ tsp horseradish sauce at one end of each portion of ham;
        then add apple slice on top of sauce.
Roll   each ham slice into small, tight roll and fasten with toothpick.
Serve   cold or hot as appetizer.

To heat, place the filled rolls in a warm oven for a few minutes, or
sauté them lightly in skillet with a small amount of margarine or oil.

ITALY # ANISE BREAD

SERVINGS: 24 slices
TIME NEEDED: 30 minutes, plus baking time

INGREDIENTS

1 egg
2 egg whites
⅔ cup sugar
¼ cup presifted cake flour

1 tsp anise seeds
pinch of nutmeg
1 egg white

EQUIPMENT

medium bowl   beater   cookie sheet, lightly greased or nonstick
bread loaf pan, lightly greased or nonstick   very sharp slicing
knife

PREPARATION

Preheat   oven at 375°F.

Combine   whole egg in bowl with 2 egg whites and sugar, beating
thoroughly for 10 minutes.

Add   flour gradually, blending gently until completely mixed;
then add anise seeds and nutmeg, and mix well.

Beat   remaining egg white until stiff and fold very gently into
batter.

Dust   loaf pan lightly with flour.

Bake   bread 20 minutes in loaf pan (or until tester comes out
dry); then remove pan from oven but do *not* turn oven off.

Loosen   bread from pan, remove it, slice thinly; then spread slices
on cookie sheet.

Bake   about 2 minutes, or until golden on top; then turn slices
over and repeat toasting process.

KOREA   **PICKLED CUCUMBERS**

SERVINGS: 6–10 (1 qt)
TIME NEEDED: 15 minutes, plus marinating time

INGREDIENTS

3 medium cucumbers
¾ tsp salt
⅛ tsp cayenne pepper
dash of ground ginger (or if
    desired, for texture add
    ¼–½ tsp chopped ginger)

1 large scallion, chopped
1 small garlic clove, minced
⅓ cup water

EQUIPMENT

large bowl   chopper   plastic wrap   deep container or jar with lid

PREPARATION

Wash   cucumbers thoroughly and slice lengthwise into halves,
    then cut each slice into pieces ½ inch wide.

Place   cucumber pieces in bowl and sprinkle with ¼ tsp salt. Stir
    gently to spread salt.

Wait   10 minutes; then wash pieces well and drain.

Add   cayenne pepper, ginger, scallion, garlic, remaining salt,
    and water to cucumbers.

Mix   well, cover bowl with plastic wrap, and set in warm place.

Marinate   48 hours (stir mixture 2 to 3 times each day).

Transfer   pickles to deep container or jar; cover with liquid and
    then refrigerate.

Keep covered in refrigerator. Serve cold, ideally within a week;
otherwise cucumber pieces lose their crispness.

LEBANON   **PICKLED STUFFED PEPPERS**

SERVINGS: 6
TIME NEEDED: 30 minutes, plus pickling time

INGREDIENTS

6 medium green peppers
1 qt water
2½ cups finely chopped
   cabbage
½ cup chopped carrots

½ cup chopped celery
1 large garlic clove
3 Tbs salt
1⅓ cups vinegar

EQUIPMENT

chopper   medium bowl   toothpicks or needle and thread
large-mouthed glass jar with lid

PREPARATION

Wash   green peppers thoroughly. Then slice off tops carefully, and widely enough to serve as "caps"; remove seeds.

Boil   water, then set aside to cool.

Combine cabbage, carrots, and celery; mix thoroughly.

Stuff   peppers very tightly with vegetable mixture.

Replace tops on peppers and secure with toothpicks or thread.

Place   peppers in jar with tops facing up.

Insert   garlic clove in center among peppers.

Add   salt to 3 cups boiled water in bowl; stir well to dissolve salt. Then add vinegar.

Pour   vinegar mixture into jar to cover peppers.

Seal   jar very tightly.

Set aside 2 weeks in cool place to allow peppers to pickle.

Serve   cold as relish.

MIDDLE EAST   **TAHINI EGGPLANT DIP**

YIELD: 3 cups
TIME NEEDED: 15 minutes, plus baking time

INGREDIENTS

1 large eggplant, about 1½ lb
1 tsp vegetable oil
7 Tbs tahini (sesame paste)
2 large garlic cloves, minced
⅔ cup lemon juice

⅛ tsp salt
1 tsp olive oil (if necessary)
3–4 large sprigs parsley,
  chopped

EQUIPMENT

aluminum foil   medium baking pan   small bowl   large bowl

PREPARATION

Preheat oven to 450°F.

Wash eggplant and rub vegetable oil over entire surface; then wrap in aluminum foil.

Bake 1 to 1¼ hours on lowest rack in oven, turning eggplant occasionally until it begins to feel very mushy.

Combine tahini in small bowl with garlic, lemon juice, and salt. If tahini is too dry to blend readily with other ingredients, add 1 tsp olive oil to moisten mixture.

Put eggplant in cold water to let it cool enough to peel; discard top and skin.

Mash eggplant in large bowl; remove any tough fibers or hard portions.

Add tahini mixture to mashed eggplant and blend well.

Serve at room temperature with chopped parsley on top as garnish.

Pieces of pita bread, triangles of toast, or salt-free crackers may be used for dipping. The authentic Middle Eastern garnish for the dip is a mixture of 3 Tbs olive oil, a small chopped green pepper, and about 1 Tb pomegranate seeds, spread over the top.

NIGERIA   CHICKEN BALLS

YIELD: 6 dozen 1-inch balls
TIME NEEDED: 50 minutes

INGREDIENTS

½-lb can sweet potatoes,   *¼ tsp salt*
  drained   *¼ tsp cayenne pepper*
1 lb boneless chicken cutlets   *1 egg white*
1 small onion, minced   *vegetable oil*
1 medium tomato, chopped
  very finely

EQUIPMENT

2 small bowls   medium bowl   grinder or processor
heavy nonstick saucepan or wok, or small Dutch oven
long-handled slotted spoon   paper towels

PREPARATION

Set   oven to warm at 200°F.
Mash   sweet potatoes in small bowl.
Grind chicken cutlets into medium bowl and add sweet potatoes,
         onion, tomato, salt, and cayenne pepper.
Beat   egg white in small bowl and add to chicken mixture; blend
         until smooth.
Heat   vegetable oil, about ¼ inch deep in heavy saucepan; you
         may use minimum amount of oil needed to turn chicken balls
         golden brown without having them burn or stick.
Shape chicken mixture into 1-inch balls. To test, use slotted spoon
         to lower 1 ball into pan, and cook 3 to 4 minutes, until golden
         brown. Cut in half to check if ball is cooked all the way
         through; if not, reduce heat to allow longer cooking time and
         test another ball for desired doneness.
Cook   remaining balls a few at a time.
Drain cooked balls on paper towels and keep warm, uncovered, in
         200° oven.
Serve warm.

ROMANIA   **EGGPLANT SPREAD**

YIELD: 3 cups
TIME NEEDED: 20 minutes, plus baking and chilling time

INGREDIENTS

2 1½-lb eggplants   2 Tbs fresh lemon juice
1 small onion, chopped   1 tsp sugar
3 Tbs vegetable oil   ⅛ tsp salt

EQUIPMENT

jelly-roll pan   grinder or processor   large bowl

PREPARATION

Preheat   oven to 350°F.
Wash   eggplants and slice off tops.
Set   eggplants in jelly-roll pan with just enough water to cover
          bottom of pan so they won't stick or burn.
Bake   45 minutes, turning several times to make sure eggplants
          bake evenly, until they are soft throughout but not mushy.
Peel   skins off while hot and discard peelings. Cut eggplants
          open, remove seeds, and cut remainder into 2-inch pieces.
Grind   eggplant pieces with finest blade.
Combine   eggplant in bowl with onion, vegetable oil, lemon juice,
          sugar, and salt.
Store   24 hours, covered, in refrigerator.

Place at room temperature shortly before serving with salt-free crackers or squares of toast.

SRI LANKA **CURRIED TOMATO SPREAD**

YIELD: 1½ cups
TIME NEEDED: 10 minutes, plus simmering time

INGREDIENTS

2 Tbs vegetable oil
1 medium onion, chopped
   finely
1½ tsps curry powder

⅛ tsp salt
4 tomatoes, peeled and
   chopped

EQUIPMENT

10-inch skillet   chopper

PREPARATION

Heat vegetable oil in skillet over moderate heat.

Cook onion in hot oil until tender, but do not brown.

Add curry powder, salt, and tomatoes.

Simmer mixture about 30 minutes in skillet over low heat until it thickens, stirring occasionally to keep it from sticking or burning.

Serve hot or cold on crackers, pieces of Middle Eastern bread, or rounds of Melba toast.

UNITED STATES   **CRANBERRY-PECAN RELISH**

SERVINGS: 12–16
TIME NEEDED: 20 minutes, plus chilling time

INGREDIENTS

1 large orange
1 lemon
1 lb fresh cranberries, washed and destemmed
½ cup golden raisins, washed and destemmed

1 piece fresh ginger, about 1 inch long, slivered
½ cup honey
½ cup sugar
½ cup chopped pecans

EQUIPMENT

chopper or processor   medium bowl or refrigerator container
grater

PREPARATION

Cut   orange into segments and remove seeds.

Grate   lemon; be careful to grate only the rind and not the white layer beneath it.

Combine   orange, grated lemon rind, cranberries, raisins, and ginger in bowl.

Chop   coarsely.

Stir   honey, sugar, and pecans thoroughly into chopped mixture.

Chill   6 hours or longer to allow the flavor to mellow before serving.

UNITED STATES **HAWAIIAN MANGO CHUTNEY**

YIELD: 4 1-pt jars
TIME NEEDED: 30 minutes, plus simmering time

INGREDIENTS

7 cups green mangoes, peeled
  and sliced
3½ cups dark brown sugar
2 cups raisins
½ tsp salt
1½ cups white vinegar
1 tsp minced hot chili pepper

1½ Tbs minced garlic
1 medium onion, chopped
¼ cup peeled and chopped
  fresh ginger
1½ cups slivered almonds
1 Tb grated lemon rind

EQUIPMENT

7-qt Dutch oven   4 1-pt jars with tight lids   chopper   grater

PREPARATION

Combine   mangoes in Dutch oven with brown sugar, raisins, salt, and vinegar.

Add   chili pepper, garlic, onion, ginger, almonds, and lemon rind to mango mixture.

Boil   mixture over high heat; then reduce heat.

Simmer   1 to 1½ hours, uncovered, stirring occasionally, until mangoes are tender and chutney thickens.

Prepare   hot sterilized canning jars.

Pour   chutney into sterilized jars and seal immediately, using paraffin or any other standard canning method.

Once a jar is opened, it should be kept refrigerated. The chutney usually accompanies grilled poultry recipes or curry dishes.

UNITED STATES   ROCKY MOUNTAIN CAULIFLOWER RELISH

SERVINGS: 10–12
TIME NEEDED: 20 minutes, plus boiling, simmering, and chilling time

INGREDIENTS

½ tsp chopped chives
⅓ cup vegetable oil
⅓ cup white vinegar
¼ tsp dried celery seed
¼ tsp dried basil
⅛ tsp salt
*¼ tsp freshly ground black
    pepper*
1 medium cauliflower
2 qts boiling water
1 Tb lemon juice
1 medium onion, thinly sliced

EQUIPMENT

chopper   1-qt saucepan   3-qt saucepan   medium bowl

PREPARATION

Combine chives in 1-qt saucepan with vegetable oil, vinegar, celery seed, basil, salt, and pepper.

Heat mixture to boiling over moderate heat; then lower heat.

Simmer 5 minutes, covered.

Separate cauliflower into florets.

Pour boiling water into 3-qt saucepan

Add cauliflower florets, plus lemon juice.

Boil cauliflower 8 minutes; then add onion.

Cook 2 minutes, or until cauliflower is just tender; do not let it get soft.

Drain cauliflower and transfer to bowl.

Pour hot vinegar mixture over it and let cool to room temperature.

Chill at least 12 hours, covered, before serving.

Salads

SANTA CRUZ SALAD

SERVINGS: 6
TIME NEEDED: 30 minutes

INGREDIENTS

4 large oranges
1 Tb sugar
2 small ripe avocados

1 tsp lemon juice
½ tsp Worcestershire sauce
1 head leaf lettuce

EQUIPMENT

peeler   medium bowl   large bowl

PREPARATION

Peel   oranges, making sure to remove all white rind and membranes.

Cut   or separate oranges into quarters and then slice each quarter thinly; remove all seeds.

Sprinkle   sugar over oranges in medium bowl.

Cover   and let stand 5 minutes.

Peel   avocados and remove pits.

Cut   avocados into ½-inch cubes and set in large bowl.

Sprinkle   lemon juice over avocados and toss lightly to coat each piece with juice.

Add   Worcestershire sauce, then orange slices.

Toss   lightly and mix well, but avoid mashing avocados.

Serve   promptly on lettuce leaves on individual salad plates.

This salad does not stand well for long time because it absorbs the dressing quickly, and the resulting taste is less lively.

DOMINICAN REPUBLIC   VEGETABLE SALAD

SERVINGS: 6

TIME NEEDED: 25 minutes

INGREDIENTS

¼ cup chopped parsley

12 radishes, very thinly sliced

2 green peppers, seeded and sliced into thin strips

1 medium cucumber, peeled and sliced

1¼ cups grated carrots

1 lb tomatoes, cut into wedges

preferred salad dressing

½ lb cabbage, chopped

1 small head leaf lettuce

EQUIPMENT

chopper   grater   large bowl   medium bowl   salad bowl or platter

PREPARATION

Combine   parsley, radishes, peppers, cucumber, carrots, and tomatoes in large bowl.

Toss   lightly and add small amount of preferred salad dressing* slowly, mixing to distribute dressing evenly.

Add   small amount of preferred salad dressing to cabbage in medium bowl and set aside.

Wash   lettuce, separate leaves, and arrange them around salad bowl or platter

Spread   salad evenly over lettuce except at center.

Fill   center with dressed cabbage just before serving.

*Customarily used with the Spicy Salad Dressing (page 53).

IRAQ **ARTICHOKE SALAD**

SERVINGS: 6

TIME NEEDED: 25 minutes, plus cooling time

INGREDIENTS

¼ cup vegetable or olive oil
20 ozs canned or frozen,
 thawed artichoke hearts
2 cups green peas
3 Tbs lemon juice

⅛ tsp salt
¼ tsp black pepper
½ tsp sugar
lettuce

EQUIPMENT

12-inch skillet

PREPARATION

Heat oil in skillet over moderate heat.
Add artichoke hearts.
Cook 10 minutes.
Add green peas.
Cook 5 minutes, or until vegetables are soft.
Remove from heat and let cool.
Drain excess oil from vegetable mixture.
Add lemon juice, salt, pepper, and sugar to vegetables.

Serve as salad on bed of lettuce. It may also be served as side dish.

KOREA   # BEAN SPROUT SALAD

SERVINGS: 6–8
TIME NEEDED: 30 minutes

INGREDIENTS

2 lbs fresh or canned bean
  sprouts, drained*
⅔ cup chopped scallions
2 pimientos, chopped
2 garlic cloves, minced

4 tsps sesame seeds
1 Tb soy sauce
3 Tbs sesame or corn oil
2 Tbs white or rice vinegar
⅛ tsp black pepper

EQUIPMENT

fine sieve   chopper   large bowl   small bowl   wire whisk

PREPARATION

Mix   bean sprouts in large bowl with scallions, pimientos, and
         garlic.
Combine sesame seeds in small bowl with soy sauce, oil, vinegar,
         and pepper.
Beat   dressing gently with whisk until it thickens slightly.
Pour   dressing over bean sprout mixture and mix lightly.

*If fresh bean sprouts are used, fill 3-quart Dutch oven about three-quarters
with water. Bring to boil over moderate heat and add sprouts. Cook until
tender, about 10 minutes. Drain and run cooked sprouts under cold water.
Drain well before putting in bowl.

LEBANON   # BULGUR WHEAT SALAD

SERVINGS: 4–6

TIME NEEDED: 30 minutes, plus soaking and chilling time

INGREDIENTS

1½ cups bulgur
water
2 cups chopped fresh parsley
½ cup chopped scallions
½ cup chopped fresh mint
4 medium tomatoes, finely
  chopped

4 Tbs lemon juice
¼ tsp ground cinnamon
⅛ tsp salt
⅓ tsp black pepper
⅛ tsp paprika
¼ cup vegetable or olive oil
1 head leaf lettuce

EQUIPMENT

colander   medium bowl   small bowl   large bowl   wire whisk

PREPARATION

Rinse bulgur in colander; then soak with water to cover in medium bowl for 30 minutes, or until soft.

Drain bulgur well and transfer to large bowl.

Add parsley, scallions, mint, and tomatoes, and toss lightly.

Combine lemon juice with cinnamon, salt, pepper, and paprika in small bowl; then add oil slowly.

Beat constantly with whisk until mixture thickens; then pour the dressing over salad and toss lightly.

Chill 1 hour, to promote blending of flavors.

Toss salad lightly before serving.

This is usually served as a salad on lettuce leaves, either individually or on a large serving platter, often with quartered tomatoes or cucumber slices surrounding the bulgur-vegetable mixture. It may also be served as an appetizer or side dish.

RUSSIA   # HEALTH SALAD

SERVINGS: 6

TIME NEEDED: 20 minutes, plus chilling time

INGREDIENTS

1 large cucumber, cut into very
  thin strips
1 carrot, peeled and thinly
  sliced
1 large apple, sliced

2 cups shredded salad greens
2 tsps lemon juice
⅛ tsp salt
¼ cup yogurt
3 medium tomatoes, peeled

EQUIPMENT

sharp knife   large bowl

PREPARATION

Combine cucumber, carrot, apple, and salad greens in large bowl
         with lemon juice and salt.
Toss   salad mixture lightly but thoroughly.
Add   yogurt.
Toss   mixture lightly again.
Cut   tomatoes into quarters and arrange in circle around edges
         of salad.
Chill   until ready to serve.

This salad is traditionally prepared in a much richer version with sour
cream rather than yogurt.

SAUDI ARABIA ZESTY ORANGE SALAD

SERVINGS: 6
TIME NEEDED: 15 minutes, plus marinating time

INGREDIENTS

lettuce leaves
3 large oranges, peeled and
   very thinly sliced
2 large, sweet onions, very
   thinly sliced
3 Tbs olive oil

3 Tbs vinegar
⅛ tsp cayenne pepper
⅛ tsp salt
12 ripe, pitted olives
   (optional)*

EQUIPMENT

sharp slicing knife or slicer   medium serving bowl   small mixing
bowl   whisk or beater

PREPARATION

Line   serving bowl with a few large washed lettuce leaves.
Arrange orange and onion slices alternating over lettuce.
Beat   oil in small bowl with vinegar, cayenne pepper, and salt.
Pour   dressing evenly over salad.
Marinate 1 hour at room temperature.
Slice   drained olives in half and arrange on top of salad just
         before serving, if desired.

*While olives do not contain cholesterol, generally they are processed with
a significant amount of salt. Those watching sodium intake should read the
product label or check an ingredient reference book before selecting particular brand.

SPAIN   **MUSHROOM AND WALNUT SALAD**

SERVINGS: 6

TIME NEEDED: 20 minutes, plus chilling time

INGREDIENTS

½ garlic clove, very finely
  minced
2 Tbs wine vinegar
⅛ tsp salt
pinch of black pepper

⅛ tsp paprika
pinch of dry mustard
6 Tbs olive oil
1 cup finely chopped walnuts
3 cups sliced mushrooms

EQUIPMENT

1-pt jar with very tight lid   chopper   large bowl

PREPARATION

Combine   garlic in jar with vinegar, salt, pepper, paprika, and
           mustard.
  Blend   by shaking vigorously in tightly capped jar; add olive oil
           and shake vigorously again.
Combine   walnuts and mushrooms in bowl.
   Pour   salad dressing over mixture in bowl; toss lightly to coat
           all pieces evenly.
Refrigerate   20 minutes before serving.

If preparing this salad in advance, do not mix the dressing with the
mushrooms and walnuts, but keep the two mixtures separate in the
refrigerator. Combine them about 20 minutes before serving.

SYRIA
LIMA BEAN SALAD

SERVINGS: 2–3
TIME NEEDED: 10 minutes, plus boiling time

INGREDIENTS

1½ cups dried lima beans* *⅛ tsp salt*
1 lemon *1 Tb olive oil*
1 garlic clove, minced *lettuce (optional)*

EQUIPMENT

3-qt saucepan   strainer or colander   juicer   medium bowl

PREPARATION

Cover   beans in saucepan with water and boil until tender.
Drain   cooked beans thoroughly and transfer to bowl.
Squeeze   lemon and combine juice with garlic in bowl with cooked
            beans; add salt and olive oil.
Mix   well before serving, cold or hot.

Traditionally served either cold or hot on a bed of lettuce as a salad.
May also be served hot as a side dish.

---

*String beans are often used in place of lima beans, with the cooking time
adjusted accordingly. Half a pound of fresh beans, cut up, will yield about 1¼
cups when cooked; they should be cooked just to tenderness, and will provide
two generous or three small portions.

YEMEN   **EGGPLANT SALAD**

SERVINGS: 6–8
TIME NEEDED: 30 minutes, plus baking time

INGREDIENTS

2 lbs eggplant
1 garlic clove, minced, or ⅓
   tsp garlic powder
3–4 Tbs tahini (sesame paste)
5 Tbs lemon juice

2 medium tomatoes, sliced
3 Tbs chopped fresh parsley
2 Tbs pine nuts
lettuce (optional)

EQUIPMENT

baking sheet   food mill or processor   large bowl   chopper

PREPARATION

Preheat   oven to 400°F.

Cut   stem ends from eggplants; then place eggplants on baking sheet.

Bake   1 to 1½ hours, until eggplants are very soft and collapse.

Remove   from heat, and strip and discard skins from eggplants.

Cut   baked eggplants into pieces; process in food mill or processor, using fine blade.

Put   processed eggplant in large bowl and add garlic, tahini (amount will depend on how thin mixture is), and lemon juice.

Blend   well and check taste for seasoning, and to determine if enough tahini has been added.

Place   in large bowl and arrange tomato slices on top.

Decorate   with chopped parsley and sprinkling of pine nuts.

The salad may also be served in individual portions on a small bed of lettuce and decorated in the same fashion.

BARBADOS ## MUSHROOM SAUCE

YIELD: 1 pint
TIME NEEDED: 15 minutes, plus simmering time

INGREDIENTS

2 cups water
3–4 chicken necks
2 Tbs vegetable oil
2 medium onions, sliced
6 medium mushrooms, sliced

4 medium tomatoes, cut into
  eighths
1 tsp prepared mustard
1 Tb lime juice
⅛ tsp salt

EQUIPMENT

small saucepan   chopper   12-inch skillet

PREPARATION

Heat   1 cup water with chicken necks in saucepan.
Bring   to a boil over moderate heat; then reduce to low heat.
Simmer   30 minutes until meat on chicken necks is soft; then drain.
Pull   meat off chicken necks and chop very finely.
Heat   oil in skillet over moderate heat and add onions.
Cook   1 to 2 minutes.
Add   mushrooms and cook until tender.
Add   tomatoes to onion-mushroom mixture, plus mustard, lime
       juice, salt, 1 cup water, and chopped chicken meat.
Simmer   10 minutes, uncovered, or until sauce is slightly thickened.
Serve   hot on grilled or baked chicken, or on hot rice.

CHINA   **CAULIFLOWER-CUCUMBER SAUCE**

SERVINGS: 6–8
TIME NEEDED: 15 minutes

INGREDIENTS

2 Tbs vegetable oil
1 cup sliced cauliflower florets
½ cup peeled, sliced cucumber
1 cup chicken broth, skimmed

⅛ tsp salt
2 tsps cornstarch
2 tsps water

EQUIPMENT

10-inch skillet   saucer or small bowl

PREPARATION

Heat   oil in skillet over moderate heat and add cauliflower and cucumber.

Cook   5 minutes, stirring constantly, or until vegetables are nearly tender; then add chicken broth* and salt.

Heat   to boiling.

Combine   cornstarch with water in saucer and add to vegetable mixture.

Heat   to boiling; then lower heat.

Simmer   2 minutes.

Serve   hot over vegetable, fish, or poultry dish.

*If any chicken filling is left over from preparing Stuffed Tomatoes (page 29), it may be added to the sauce at this point.

DOMINICAN REPUBLIC   **SPICY
SALAD
DRESSING**

YIELD: 2 cups
TIME NEEDED: 15 minutes, plus chilling time

INGREDIENTS

2 Tbs very finely chopped
   onion
2 Tbs very finely chopped
   fresh parsley
½ cup chopped green pepper
1 Tb chopped sweet and sour
   pickles
3 Tbs light corn syrup

2 tsps dry mustard
1 tsp paprika
½ cup white vinegar
½ cup tomato juice
½ cup vegetable oil
½ tsp black pepper
⅛ tsp Tabasco sauce
½ tsp prepared horseradish

EQUIPMENT

chopper   large bowl   electric mixer*   jar with tight lid, large
enough to allow shaking 2 cups

PREPARATION

Combine onion, parsley, green pepper, and pickles in large bowl.
    Add corn syrup, mustard, paprika, vinegar, tomato juice, vege-
        table oil, black pepper, Tabasco sauce, and horseradish.
   Beat at low speed with electric mixer until thoroughly blended.
   Pour into jar.
   Chill until needed.

*If no mixer is available, the ingredients can be shaken vigorously in the very
tightly capped jar.

GRENADA   # TOMATO KETCHUP

YIELD: 3–4 cups
TIME NEEDED: 40 minutes, plus simmering time, and sterilizing time
if not used immediately

INGREDIENTS

3 lbs fresh tomatoes, quartered   ⅛ tsp ground nutmeg
½ cup sugar   ⅛ tsp ground ginger
½ cup malt vinegar   ¼ tsp salt
⅛ tsp ground cinnamon   ¼ tsp ground mace

EQUIPMENT

4-qt Dutch oven   food mill or similar device for very fine
straining   small preserving jars with tight lids

PREPARATION

Cook   tomatoes 10 minutes in covered Dutch oven on low heat, or
        until they soften and juice runs out.

Cook   5 to 10 minutes longer, uncovered, until tomatoes become
        very soft.

Puree   tomatoes in food mill; return processed tomatoes to Dutch
        oven.

Add   remaining ingredients.

Bring   to a boil over moderate heat; then reduce heat.

Simmer 30 minutes on low heat, uncovered, stirring until mixture
        thickens.

Prepare jars to be sterilized as for preserving and pour hot ketchup
        into jars; seal immediately by standard procedure. Store
        ketchup in refrigerator, where it can be kept for several
        weeks.

ITALY **TARRAGON VINEGAR DRESSING**

YIELD: 2 cups
TIME NEEDED: 15 minutes

INGREDIENTS

½ cup tarragon vinegar
1 Tb lemon juice
1 Tb coarsely ground black
  pepper
1½ tsps paprika
1 Tb dried oregano
1 Tb dried basil

1½ tsps Worcestershire sauce
1 cup vegetable or olive oil
2 Tbs mayonnaise or salad
  dressing*
½ oz crumbled or shredded
  cheese (Roquefort, blue, or
  special diet)

EQUIPMENT

pepper mill   medium bowl   wire whisk or beater   jar with tight
lid

PREPARATION

Blend   vinegar, lemon juice, pepper, paprika, oregano, basil, and
  Worcestershire sauce in bowl.
Add   oil (traditionally olive) slowly, while beating with whisk until
  very well blended.
Beat   mayonnaise or salad dressing into oil.
Add   cheese; beat mixture till smooth.
Pour   dressing into jar.

Make sure the jar is large enough. This recipe makes about 6 servings, and any leftover dressing can be stored in the refrigerator.

*Some low cholesterol or cholesterol-free products are now available com-
mercially.

TRINIDAD AND TOBAGO   CREOLE
SAUCE

SERVINGS: 6–8
TIME NEEDED: 40 minutes, plus simmering time

INGREDIENTS

3 Tbs vegetable oil
1 large onion, chopped
1 large green pepper, seeded and chopped
2 large tomatoes, peeled and chopped

⅛ tsp dried thyme
⅛ tsp salt
⅛ tsp black pepper
½ cup water
1 tsp lime juice
¼ tsp sugar

EQUIPMENT

chopper   4-qt Dutch oven

PREPARATION

Heat   oil in Dutch oven over moderate heat.
Cook   onion and green pepper in hot oil until light brown, stirring occasionally; then add tomatoes, thyme, salt, and black pepper to hot mixture.
Cook   until mixture is soft and sauce has thickened, stirring to keep it from sticking or scorching.
Add   water, lime juice, and sugar.
Simmer   5 minutes over low heat, stirring thoroughly before serving.

This sauce is often served over baked fish and other seafood dishes, and with grilled or roast meat or poultry.

UNITED STATES　**COUNTRY INN SAUCE**

SERVINGS: 2–4
TIME NEEDED: 10 minutes

INGREDIENTS

1 Tb margarine	¾ cup yogurt
1½ Tbs flour	1 Tb very finely chopped
pinch of salt	chives or scallion
½ cup clear chicken broth,	
skimmed	

EQUIPMENT
chopper　small saucepan　small bowl

PREPARATION

Melt　margarine in saucepan.

Stir　flour into margarine, then salt and chicken broth.

Cook　1 minute, stirring constantly, or until mixture thickens and starts to boil.

Pour　yogurt into small bowl; stir in 2 Tbs thickened sauce and blend well.

Remove　pan with boiled sauce from heat.

Add　yogurt to hot sauce slowly and blend thoroughly; do not reheat.

Pour　sauce on chicken or other entrée and garnish with sprinkling of chives or scallion.

For best results, the sauce should be prepared just before it is to be served. This sauce goes particularly well with Country Inn Chicken (page 96) and with grilled or roast poultry.

UNITED STATES   **RED CURRANT**
SALAD
DRESSING

SERVINGS: 12
TIME NEEDED: 10 minutes

INGREDIENTS

1 cup olive oil   ¼ tsp ground white pepper
¼ cup tarragon vinegar   ¼ tsp sugar
pinch of salt   ⅓ cup red currant jelly*

EQUIPMENT
small bowl   whisk   cruet or jar with tight lid

PREPARATION
Blend   olive oil with vinegar, salt, pepper, and sugar in bowl; beat
        well with whisk.
Add   currant jelly, and continue blending well with whisk.
Pour   dressing into cruet to serve immediately, or store in tight jar
        in refrigerator until needed.

The dressing is particularly appropriate for light summer salads such
as fruit salads.

*If currant jelly is unavailable, apple or plum jelly can also be used.

CHINA   **PUMPKIN SOUP**

SERVINGS: 6–8
TIME NEEDED: 10 minutes, plus simmering time

INGREDIENTS

2 1-lb cans unseasoned   ⅛ tsp salt
    pumpkin*   ¼ tsp black pepper
5 cups chicken broth, skimmed
1 medium onion, very finely
    grated

EQUIPMENT

3-qt Dutch oven or heavy saucepan   grater or fine chopper

PREPARATION

Stir   pumpkin in Dutch oven until smooth.
Add   chicken broth gradually, stirring to eliminate lumps; add
        onion, salt, and pepper.
Heat   to boiling over moderate heat; then lower heat.
Simmer   20 minutes, partially covered; stir occasionally to keep
        smooth and prevent sticking.

The soup should have the consistency of creamed tomato soup. If it
becomes too thick during simmering, add a little more chicken stock;
then stir the mixture well before removing from the heat.

*Check the label on the can to make sure the pumpkin is unseasoned. Do not
use canned pie filling, which is usually preseasoned. If fresh pumpkin is used,
6–7 cups cooked pumpkin will be needed.

DENMARK   ## CAULIFLOWER SOUP

SERVINGS: 6

TIME NEEDED: 30 minutes, plus simmering time

INGREDIENTS

3¼ cups water
1 medium-to-large head
  cauliflower, separated into
  florets
1 large onion, sliced thinly
2 Tbs minced celery tops
2 Tbs margarine

2 Tbs flour
1 cup chicken broth, skimmed
⅛ tsp salt
¼ tsp white pepper
1 cup yogurt
ground nutmeg
Madeira or sherry (optional)

EQUIPMENT

3-qt saucepan   blender   medium bowl or heatproof container

PREPARATION

Heat   2 cups water to boiling in saucepan and add cauliflower,
        onion, and celery tops. Boil 1 minute; then reduce to low
        heat.

Simmer 10 minutes, covered, or until cauliflower is tender; then
        remove from heat and cool slightly.

Pour   part of vegetables and water into blender. Do *not* fill more
        than one-third of the way, and make sure that mixture is
        not too hot; otherwise container may explode.

Puree   until smooth; pour into bowl and repeat until all vegetables
        and water are pureed.

Melt   margarine in saucepan and blend in flour gradually, stirring
        well until mixture becomes smooth and bubbles form; then
        lower heat.

Add   1¼ cups water gradually, stirring constantly until smooth.

Heat   to boiling, stirring continuously, then add pureed vegeta-
        bles, chicken broth, salt, and pepper.

Heat   to a vigorous boil; then turn off heat. Leave pan on warm
        burner, and slowly add yogurt and blend well; do not let
        boil.

Serve   hot or cold with sprinkling of nutmeg, and 1 or 2 Tbs wine
        added to each portion, if desired.

HUNGARY   ## PLUM SOUP

SERVINGS: 6

TIME NEEDED: 20 minutes, plus simmering and chilling time

INGREDIENTS

5 cups water	2 Tbs sugar
1½ lbs plums, pitted and sliced	1 cup yogurt (optional)
1 Tb flour	

EQUIPMENT

medium saucepan   small bowl   medium bowl or refrigerator container

PREPARATION

Heat   water and plums to boiling; then lower heat.

Simmer   20 to 30 minutes, until plums are soft and almost mushy.

Blend   flour in small bowl with a little of the plum soup, stirring until smooth.

Add   flour mixture to plum soup in saucepan, stirring continuously until soup thickens slightly.

Stir   sugar into hot soup.

Boil   5 minutes; then set aside to cool.

Pour   cooled soup into medium bowl for refrigerating.

Serve   thoroughly chilled.

Various kinds of cold soups, including those made with fruit, are highly popular in Hungary during the summer, when local produce, especially cherries, plums, and apricots, is abundant. Frequently heavy sour cream is mixed into the cold soup just before serving. If sour cream is not allowed in your diet, yogurt can be substituted for a less rich version of the authentic recipe.

INDONESIA   **MIXED VEGETABLE SOUP**

SERVINGS: 6–8
TIME NEEDED: 30 minutes, plus boiling and simmering time

INGREDIENTS

2 Tbs vegetable oil
1 garlic clove, chopped very
  fine
½ cup diced raw chicken*
⅛ tsp salt
¼ tsp black pepper
¼ tsp ground ginger
1 bay leaf
½ cup sliced carrots
½ cup fresh green beans, cut
  into 1-inch pieces

½ medium onion, sliced
2 Tbs chopped celery
½ tomato, chopped
½ cup shredded cabbage
6 cups chicken broth,
  skimmed*
½ cup uncooked thin noodles†
½ cup cubed bean curd
  (optional)

EQUIPMENT

chopper   4-qt Dutch oven   shredder or processor

PREPARATION

Heat   vegetable oil in Dutch oven over moderate heat; add garlic
        and cook until tender.
Add   chicken, salt, pepper, ginger, and bay leaf.
Cook   until chicken is done.
Add   carrots, green beans, onion, and celery.
Cook   5 minutes, stirring occasionally.
Add   tomato, cabbage, chicken broth, and noodles.
Heat   soup to boiling; then reduce to low heat.
Simmer 30 minutes, covered, or until vegetables are tender. Then
        add bean curd, if desired.

*The soup is also made with beef and beef broth.
†In diets with egg consumption restricted, noodles made without egg may be
used.

MADAGASCAR VEGETABLE SOUP

SERVINGS: 6
TIME NEEDED: 25 minutes, plus simmering time

INGREDIENTS

1½ lbs lean veal bones
½ tsp salt
1 qt water
1 large tomato, peeled and chopped
2 small potatoes, peeled and diced
2 small carrots, pared and chopped

½ small white turnip, peeled and diced
½ cup fresh string beans, cut into 1-inch pieces
1 scallion or ½ small leek
pinch of black pepper

EQUIPMENT

4-qt Dutch oven   3-qt saucepan   parer   chopper   blender

PREPARATION

Place bones in Dutch oven with salt and water.
Bring to a boil over moderate heat; then lower heat.
Simmer 1 hour, covered.
Add tomato and potatoes.
Simmer 30 minutes.
Add carrots, turnip, string beans, scallion or leek, and pepper.
Simmer 1 hour, or until vegetables are very soft.
Remove and discard veal bones.
Cool soup slightly.
Pour part of warm soup gradually into blender container. Do *not* fill more than one-third of the way, and make sure that soup is not too hot; otherwise container may explode. Puree soup until smooth.
Pour pureed soup into saucepan.
Puree rest of soup; fill blender only one-third of the way at a time.
Rewarm soup in saucepan over low heat before serving.

The soup is equally delicious if served chilled.

MEXICO   **APPLE SOUP**

SERVINGS: 6–8

TIME NEEDED: 15 minutes, plus simmering time

INGREDIENTS

2 Tbs margarine

1 medium onion, chopped

1 heaping Tb flour

¾ cup tomato juice

1½ qts chicken broth, skimmed

⅛ tsp black pepper

¾ cup apple wine*

2 large firm crisp apples,
   peeled and cut in ½-inch
   cubes

2 Tbs chopped parsley

EQUIPMENT

chopper   3-qt saucepan or soup pot   wire whisk   peeler

PREPARATION

Melt   margarine in saucepan over low heat.

Add   onion and cook until tender, stirring occasionally for even cooking; then add flour gradually, blending well with whisk until smooth.

Cook   3 to 4 minutes, stirring occasionally to keep lumps from forming and to prevent scorching.

Stir   tomato juice into flour mixture, blending until smooth; add chicken broth and pepper.

Simmer 10 minutes with lid partially covering pot.

Add   apple wine and apple cubes to soup, stirring until soup is well blended and thoroughly hot.

Serve   hot, with parsley as garnish.

*Hard apple cider, if not too sweet or highly fermented, may be substituted.

NORWAY

COLD SOUR SOUP

SERVINGS: 6–8
TIME NEEDED: 45 minutes

INGREDIENTS

4½ cups water
¼ cup uncooked rice
½ cup raisins
2¼ cups yogurt

2 tsps grated lemon rind
2¼ cups raspberry juice
1–2 Tbs lemon juice (optional)*

EQUIPMENT

2-qt saucepan   medium bowl   grater   strainer

PREPARATION

Boil water in saucepan over moderate heat.
Add rice.
Cook 10 to 15 minutes, covered, or until rice is tender.
Add raisins.
Cook 5 minutes, or until raisins become plump.
Drain liquid and discard.
Combine yogurt in bowl with lemon rind and raspberry juice, and lemon juice if desired.
Blend yogurt mixture well.
Add rice mixture and stir well.
Serve chilled or at room temperature.

*Lemon juice may be added if a slightly more tart taste is preferred.

SPAIN   **POTATO AND CARROT SOUP**

SERVINGS: 8–10
TIME NEEDED: 25 minutes, plus simmering time

INGREDIENTS

3 Tbs margarine
2 medium onions, chopped
6 medium carrots, scraped and
    chopped
2 medium leeks, chopped
3 medium potatoes, peeled and
    diced

1 bay leaf
¼ tsp salt
¼ tsp black pepper
6 cups chicken broth, skimmed

EQUIPMENT

chopper   scraper   parer   4-qt Dutch oven   blender
3-qt saucepan

PREPARATION

Melt	margarine in Dutch oven over moderate heat.
Add	onions, carrots, and leeks.
Cook	until tender.
Add	potatoes, bay leaf, salt, pepper, and chicken broth.
Heat	to boiling; then reduce heat.
Simmer	20 minutes, partially covered, or until potatoes are tender.
Remove	bay leaf and discard.
Pour	part of mixture gradually into blender container. Do *not* fill more than one-third of the way, and make sure mixture is not too hot; otherwise container may explode. Puree mixture.
Transfer	pureed soup to saucepan and continue processing until all the soup is pureed.
Rewarm	before serving.

If the soup is kept in the refrigerator and thickens too much, it can be thinned with additional chicken broth during reheating.

UNITED STATES **VERMONT GREEN MOUNTAIN ZUCCHINI SOUP**

SERVINGS: 6

TIME NEEDED: 25 minutes, plus simmering time

INGREDIENTS

1½ lbs zucchini	¼ tsp dried oregano
6 cups chicken broth, skimmed	⅛ tsp salt
1 medium onion, sliced	¼ tsp black pepper
¼ tsp chervil	¾ cup frozen peas

EQUIPMENT

7-qt Dutch oven   blender

PREPARATION

Wash zucchini thoroughly and remove ends; then cut into ¼-inch-thick slices.

Combine chicken broth, onion, chervil, oregano, salt, and pepper in Dutch oven.

Simmer for a few minutes; then bring to a boil and add zucchini.

Simmer 15 minutes over low heat; then add frozen peas and simmer until zucchini and peas are soft. Remove from heat and let cool slightly.

Fill blender one-third of the way with soup; do *not* fill any more than this, and make sure that soup is not too hot; otherwise blender container may explode. Puree soup. Repeat procedure until all the soup is pureed.

Reheat soup in Dutch oven before serving, or serve chilled.

ALBANIA **POTATO-CARROT CASSEROLE**

SERVINGS: 6–8
TIME NEEDED: 25 minutes, plus baking time

INGREDIENTS

2¼ qts water
2 lbs potatoes, peeled and
   thinly sliced
4 medium carrots, pared and
   thinly sliced
¼ tsp salt
½ tsp freshly ground black
   pepper

4 large tomatoes, peeled and
   sliced
3 garlic cloves, minced
¼ cup chopped fresh parsley
2 cups chicken stock, skimmed
vegetable or olive oil for
   basting

EQUIPMENT

3-qt pot   parer   3-qt casserole or Dutch oven   pepper mill
large bowl

PREPARATION

Preheat   oven to 350°F.

Heat   water to boiling in pot over moderate heat.

Boil   potatoes and carrots 3 minutes in the hot water; then drain.

Arrange   potatoes and carrots on bottom of greased or nonstick casserole or Dutch oven.

Sprinkle   ⅛ tsp salt and ¼ tsp pepper on vegetables.

Combine   tomatoes in large bowl with garlic, parsley, and remainder of salt and pepper.

Spread   tomato mixture over potatoes and carrots.

Add   chicken stock.

Bake   45 minutes, uncovered.

Baste   top of vegetables with sprinkling of oil (traditionally olive).

Bake   20 minutes, or until vegetables are tender.

ARGENTINA   **CORN SUPREME**

SERVINGS 8

TIME NEEDED: 20 minutes, plus simmering time

INGREDIENTS

2 Tbs olive oil	¼ tsp ground cinnamon
1 medium onion, finely chopped	1½ tsp paprika
	1 ripe tomato, chopped
1 garlic clove, finely minced	½ cup low-fat milk
1 small green pepper, chopped	4 cups frozen or canned
⅛ tsp salt	whole-kernel corn, or 12 ears
1 bay leaf	fresh corn, grated
¼ tsp black pepper	

EQUIPMENT

large saucepan   chopper   grater (if fresh corn used)

PREPARATION

Heat	oil in saucepan.
Add	onion and garlic.
Cook	until onion is tender.
Add	green pepper.
Cook	2 minutes.
Add	salt, bay leaf, black pepper, cinnamon, and paprika, and mix well.
Cook	1 minute.
Add	tomato.
Simmer	10 minutes.
Add	milk and corn.
Simmer	15 minutes at low heat (more time may be required if fresh corn is used), stirring frequently until corn is tender.
Serve	hot or cold.

AUSTRIA   ## CREAMED CUCUMBER

SERVINGS: 6

TIME NEEDED: 35 minutes

INGREDIENTS

4 Tbs margarine
2 Tbs flour
1 cup chicken broth, skimmed
⅛ tsp salt

¼ tsp black pepper
3 medium cucumbers, peeled
   and very thinly sliced
1 cup yogurt

EQUIPMENT

2-qt saucepan   wire whisk

PREPARATION

Melt	margarine in saucepan over moderate heat.
Combine	flour with margarine, stirring constantly with whisk until thoroughly blended (about 2 minutes).
Add	chicken broth very slowly, beating constantly to keep mixture smooth.
Bring	to boil at moderate heat; then lower heat.
Simmer	2 minutes.
Add	salt, pepper, and cucumbers.
Cook	over low heat 10 minutes, or until cucumbers are tender; then remove from heat.
Stir	yogurt slowly into cucumber mixture, blending to keep from curdling.
Cook	3 to 5 minutes over very low heat; do *not* boil, or yogurt may curdle.

BAHAMAS   # PEAS AND RICE

SERVINGS: 6–8

TIME NEEDED: 20 minutes, plus boiling and simmering time

INGREDIENTS

6 cups water

1 cup dried pigeon peas

1 Tb vegetable oil

1 small onion, very finely
   chopped

½ cup canned tomatoes,
   chopped

⅛ tsp salt

½ tsp black pepper

¼ tsp dried thyme

2 cups uncooked long-grain
   rice

EQUIPMENT

4-qt Dutch oven   chopper   10-inch skillet

PREPARATION

Place   water and pigeon peas in Dutch oven.

Bring   to boil over moderate heat; then reduce to low heat.

Simmer   1 hour, covered, or until peas are tender.

Heat   oil in skillet and add onion.

Sauté   until onion is golden.

Add   tomatoes, salt, pepper, and thyme.

Cook   5 minutes.

Add   onion mixture to peas; then add rice.

Bring   to boil over moderate heat; then reduce to low heat.

Simmer   about 30 minutes, or until liquid is absorbed and rice is tender. If liquid is gone before rice is cooked, add a little more water.

CHILE   **PEPPERS WITH CORN STUFFING**

SERVINGS: 6
TIME NEEDED: 45 minutes, plus baking time

INGREDIENTS

6 large green sweet peppers
2 medium onions
3 Tbs vegetable oil
¼ tsp nutmeg
¼ tsp cumin
¼ tsp cayenne pepper
4 medium tomatoes, peeled
    and chopped

2 cups grated, fresh corn
    (about 8 ears) or frozen corn
½ cup crumbled fresh bread
½ cup milk
1 tsp sugar
⅛ tsp salt
2 Tbs dry bread crumbs
1 cup water

EQUIPMENT

paper towels   12-inch skillet   grater   chopper   small bowl
1½-qt baking dish

PREPARATION

Preheat	oven to 350°F.
Slice	tops off peppers (keep the tops) and remove seeds and wash.
Place	peppers open end down on paper towels to drain.
Chop	any usable parts of pepper tops, and onions.
Heat	2 Tbs oil in skillet over moderate heat.
Add	pepper-onion mixture.
Cook	5 minutes, stirring occasionally until tender.
Add	nutmeg, cumin, and cayenne pepper.
Cook	1 minute, stirring vigorously.
Add	tomatoes to skillet; cook until mixture thickens.
Add	corn and blend well.
Combine	crumbled bread in small bowl with milk, and mix well; then add to skillet, along with sugar and salt.
Fill	peppers with corn mixture and arrange them in baking dish.
Sprinkle	bread crumbs over tops.
Drizzle	1 Tb oil over bread crumbs and add water to the pan.
Bake	45 minutes, or until peppers are done but stuffing is still moist and only lightly browned.

ITALY   # CARROTS WITH WINE

SERVINGS: 6
TIME NEEDED: 40 minutes, plus simmering time

INGREDIENTS

2 Tbs margarine	1 Tb sugar
1½ lbs carrots, scraped and	½ cup Marsala or other sweet
sliced into 3-inch sticks	wine*
⅛ tsp salt	⅓ cup water
¼ tsp black pepper	¼ cup chopped parsley

EQUIPMENT

scraper   10-inch heavy skillet   chopper

PREPARATION

Melt margarine in skillet over moderate heat and add carrots; toss well to coat evenly with margarine.

Sauté 5 minutes, stirring occasionally.

Sprinkle salt, pepper, and sugar over carrots; blend well.

Add wine and water.

Heat to boiling; then reduce to very low heat.

Simmer 20 to 25 minutes, covered, or until carrots reach desired tenderness.

Cook over high heat, uncovered, until liquid is reduced and a slightly thick sauce remains; stir lightly to prevent burning or sticking.

Sprinkle parsley over carrots.

Serve immediately, while hot. (On standing, sauce tends to dry out or be absorbed by the carrots.)

*Traditionally Marsala is preferred.

KUWAIT ## ROSEWATER RICE

SERVINGS: 6–8
TIME NEEDED: 20 minutes, plus simmering time

INGREDIENTS

2 cups uncooked long-grain
   rice
6 cups boiling water
¼ cup rosewater
½ tsp saffron

½ tsp ground cardamom
⅓ cup sugar
1 Tb margarine
⅛ tsp salt

EQUIPMENT

2-qt saucepan   small bowl   colander or sieve

PREPARATION

Add	rice to boiling water in saucepan and then lower heat.
Simmer	10 to 12 minutes, covered; rice should be not quite tender.
Combine	rosewater in small bowl with saffron and cardamom.
Drain	cooked rice in colander; then add sugar and toss mixture in colander.
Melt	margarine in saucepan and return rice to pan.
Add	rosewater-and-spice mixture; blend well but lightly.
Sprinkle	salt over rice mixture and toss well.
Reheat	over low heat until rice is tender; stir occasionally to keep it from sticking.
Serve	hot as side dish.

In Kuwait this dish is usually served with fish or lamb.

LESOTHO   # CURRIED EGGPLANT

SERVINGS: 6
TIME NEEDED: 40 minutes

INGREDIENTS

3 Tbs vegetable oil

1 medium onion, chopped

1 1-lb eggplant, peeled and
   diced

⅛ tsp salt

⅛ tsp black pepper

½ tsp curry powder

3 large boiling potatoes, peeled
   and cubed (optional)

EQUIPMENT

chopper   3-qt saucepan or Dutch oven

PREPARATION

Heat oil in saucepan over moderate heat.

Add onion to hot oil and cook, stirring until tender.

Add eggplant, salt, pepper, and curry powder.

Cook 15 to 20 minutes, stirring to blend well, or until eggplant is
       tender.

Parboiled potatoes may be added to the eggplant mixture during the
last few minutes of cooking so that both vegetables are done at the
same time.

MONACO   **RATATOUILLE**

SERVINGS: 6–8
TIME NEEDED: 25 minutes, plus simmering times

INGREDIENTS

2 Tbs olive oil
1 large onion, thinly sliced
3 medium garlic cloves, minced
2 green peppers, seeded and
 cut into ⅜-inch slices
3 large zucchini or similar
 squash, cut into ¼-inch
 slices

1 medium eggplant, coarsely
 diced
3 Tbs drained capers
1 28-oz can tomatoes, drained
¼ tsp black pepper
⅛ tsp salt
1 tsp dried basil

EQUIPMENT

7-qt Dutch oven   fine sieve

PREPARATION

Heat   oil in Dutch oven and sauté onion and garlic until softened.
Add   green peppers, squash, eggplant, capers, and tomatoes.
Mix   thoroughly over moderately high heat and add black pepper, salt, and basil.
Simmer   50 minutes, covered, over medium heat; stir occasionally to break up large pieces of tomatoes.
Simmer   15 to 30 minutes, uncovered, over moderately high heat until mixture thickens as desired.
Serve   hot or cold.

POLAND TOMATOES STUFFED WITH BARLEY

SERVINGS: 6
TIME NEEDED: 45 minutes, plus simmering and baking time

INGREDIENTS

2 cups water
1 oz dried European
  mushrooms
1 Tb vegetable oil or
  margarine
1 medium onion, chopped
½ cup pearl barley (or groats
  or rice)

6 medium tomatoes
6 Tbs yogurt
3 Tbs grated cheese
  (preferably low-cholesterol,
  low-fat)
2 Tbs chopped fresh dill

EQUIPMENT

small saucepan   chopper   2-qt saucepan   1½-qt baking dish
very sharp slicing knife

PREPARATION

Bring	water to boil in small saucepan over high heat; then reduce to low heat.
Add	mushrooms.
Simmer	15 minutes, covered.
Remove	mushrooms and drain; reserve liquid.
Chop	mushrooms very finely.
Heat	oil in 2-qt saucepan over moderate heat.
Sauté	onion until light brown.
Add	barley, 1½ cups of the reserved mushroom liquid, and chopped mushrooms; stir well.
Simmer	about 1 hour, until barley is tender. If it becomes too dry while simmering, add more mushroom liquid.
Heat	oven to 350°F.
Slice	tops carefully from tomatoes; make slices thick enough to keep tops intact so they can be replaced for baking.
Scoop	out insides of tomatoes and stuff with barley mixture.
Reset	tops on tomatoes and set them upright in baking dish.
Spread	1 Tb yogurt across top of each tomato; then sprinkle each with a portion of cheese and dill.
Bake	30 minutes.

QATAR   **LENTILS WITH TOMATOES**

SERVINGS: 6–8

TIME NEEDED: 45 minutes, plus simmering time

INGREDIENTS

2 cups lentils

2½ qts boiling water

2 Tbs vegetable oil

2 onions, very thinly sliced

1 medium green pepper, cut
   into strips

3 pimientos, cut into strips

2 garlic cloves, minced

8 canned tomatoes, quartered,
   or 8 medium fresh tomatoes,
   peeled and quartered

⅛ tsp salt

⅛ tsp black pepper

pinch of cumin (optional)

EQUIPMENT

large saucepan   6-qt Dutch oven   large strainer

PREPARATION

Rinse   lentils with cold water.

Add   lentils to boiling water in saucepan and boil 20 minutes at high heat.

Heat   oil over high heat in Dutch oven until oil sizzles; then lower to moderate heat.

Sauté   onions, green peppers, pimientos, and garlic in Dutch oven.

Add   tomatoes to vegetable mixture when onions have become soft; do not let onions get mushy.

Drain   cooked lentils and add to vegetable mixture; add salt and black pepper, and cumin if desired.

Simmer   15 minutes, uncovered, over low heat.

SRI LANKA   **SEASONED RICE**

SERVINGS: 6

TIME NEEDED: 20 minutes, plus simmering time

INGREDIENTS

1 Tb margarine	*1 cinnamon stick*
1 medium onion, chopped	*6 cloves*
1 cup uncooked long-grain rice	*4 cardamom seeds, slightly*
¼ tsp saffron	*crushed*
2 cups chicken broth, skimmed	*⅛ tsp salt*

EQUIPMENT

chopper   2-qt saucepan

PREPARATION

Melt   margarine in saucepan over moderate heat.

Add   onion and sauté until lightly browned.

Add   rice and saffron.

Cook   2 minutes, stirring constantly.

Add   chicken broth, cinnamon stick, cloves, cardamom seeds, and salt.

Heat   to boiling; then reduce heat to low. Stir to prevent sticking or burning.

Simmer   20 to 25 minutes, covered, or until liquid is absorbed and rice is tender.

SWEDEN   # SWEET-AND-SOUR
RED CABBAGE

SERVINGS: 6
TIME NEEDED: 30 minutes, plus baking time

INGREDIENTS

2½–3 lbs red cabbage
⅓ cup water
3 Tbs margarine
1 Tb sugar
⅛ tsp salt

⅓ cup white or cider vinegar
¼ cup jelly (currant, apple, or
 plum)
1 small tart apple, peeled and
 grated

EQUIPMENT

cutting board   corer   sharp slicing knife or processor   5-qt Dutch oven or ovenproof casserole   grater

PREPARATION

Preheat   oven to 325°F.
Remove   tough outer leaves from cabbage and wash remaining cabbage in cold water.
Cut   cabbage in half, slicing from top to bottom; remove core completely and shred cabbage into thin slices.
Heat   water to boiling in Dutch oven; add margarine, sugar, salt, and vinegar.
Add   cabbage, mixing lightly but well, and heat to boiling.
Cook   2 hours in oven, covered, checking occasionally to see whether cabbage has dried out and needs more water.
Stir   jelly and apple into cabbage.
Cook   10 to 15 minutes longer, covered, until apple is soft.
Serve   hot.

UNITED STATES **BARLEY
MÈRE JACQUES**

SERVINGS: 2–3
TIME NEEDED: 30 minutes, plus baking time

INGREDIENTS

2 Tbs margarine   1 cup pearl barley
3 Tbs chopped onion   1–1½ cups chicken broth,
⅓ cup sliced mushrooms   skimmed

EQUIPMENT

1½-qt flameproof casserole with cover   chopper

PREPARATION

Preheat oven to 350°F.
  Melt   margarine in casserole over low heat.
   Add   onion and mushrooms.
  Cook   until tender; then add barley and mix well.
  Cook   at moderate heat, stirring occasionally, until barley is
         lightly browned.
   Add   ⅓ cup chicken broth.
  Bake   20 minutes with casserole covered.
   Add   ⅓ cup chicken broth.
  Bake   30 minutes, uncovered.
   Add   ⅓ cup chicken broth.
  Bake   20 minutes, or until barley is tender; add more chicken
         broth if necessary to keep barley from drying out.

BULGARIA

BAKED FISH
WITH VEGETABLES

SERVINGS: 6–8
TIME NEEDED: 30 minutes, plus baking time

INGREDIENTS

1 small celery heart, cut into
   1-inch pieces
1 lb carrots, pared and thinly
   sliced
1 lb tomatoes, diced
3 medium onions, sliced
2 garlic cloves, minced
1/8 tsp salt
1/4 tsp black pepper

2 1/2 lbs fish fillets (flounder,
   cod, shad, haddock)
1/2 cup dry white wine
2 bay leaves
1 cup fine fresh bread crumbs
1/2 cup ground walnuts
   (optional)*
2 Tbs vegetable oil
3 lemons, thinly sliced

EQUIPMENT

grinder or processor (optional)   7-qt Dutch oven

PREPARATION

Preheat   oven to 400°F.
Place   all prepared vegetables in Dutch oven and sprinkle garlic,
salt, and pepper over them.
Arrange   fish fillets (use a mixture of at least two kinds of firm fish)
over vegetables; then pour wine over fish.
Add   bay leaves.
Combine   bread crumbs with walnuts and cover fish with layer of
crumb mixture; sprinkle oil over mixture.
Arrange   lemon slices on top of crumb mixture.
Bake   1 hour, uncovered, or until fish flakes easily and vegeta-
bles are tender.

*If nuts are not used, add 1/2 cup additional bread crumbs.

CAMEROON　　　　**FISH STEW**

SERVINGS: 6–8

TIME NEEDED: 45 minutes, plus simmering time

INGREDIENTS

2–3 cups uncooked rice

⅓ cup vegetable oil

2 medium onions, sliced

3 Tbs tomato paste

2½ lbs fish fillets (halibut, swordfish, firm fish), cut in large pieces

2 large carrots, sliced

2 small sweet potatoes, peeled and cut into 1-inch cubes

½ lb cabbage, shredded

5 ozs frozen okra

1 qt water

EQUIPMENT

4-qt saucepan

PREPARATION

Cook　rice.

Heat　oil in saucepan.

Add　onions to hot oil and heat until onions turn yellow; do not brown them.

Add　tomato paste and fish.

Cook　25 to 30 minutes, covered, over low heat.

Layer　carrots, sweet potatoes, and cabbage on fish.

Add　okra and water.

Simmer　about 30 minutes.

Serve　in center of individual bowls of cooked rice.

CYPRUS   **FISH BAKED WITH TOMATOES**

SERVINGS: 6

TIME NEEDED: 20 minutes, plus baking time

INGREDIENTS

1 Tb olive oil

4 large tomatoes, peeled and sliced

2 large onions, sliced

3½–4 lbs sea trout, sea bass, or striped bass

1 Tb lemon juice

⅛ tsp salt

¼ tsp black pepper

2 Tbs chopped fresh parsley

6 pitted black olives, cut in halves

½ cup dry white wine

4 Tbs vegetable or olive oil

1 large lemon, thinly sliced

EQUIPMENT

large, shallow baking pan (oiled or nonstick)

PREPARATION

Preheat   oven to 350°F.

Brush   olive oil over surface of baking pan, or use nonstick pan.

Arrange   half of tomato and onion slices on bottom of baking pan.

Rub   fish on both sides with lemon juice.

Mix   salt and pepper and rub over fish.

Place   fish on top of vegetables in baking pan.

Arrange   rest of tomato and onion slices and parsley on top of fish.

Arrange   olive halves in row atop fish.

Pour   wine over fish, along with oil (traditionally olive).

Arrange   lemon slices in row atop fish.

Bake   30 to 40 minutes, uncovered, or until fish flakes easily with a fork.

IRELAND   # SALMON IN WINE SAUCE

SERVINGS: 6

TIME NEEDED: 55 minutes, plus baking time

INGREDIENTS

3 medium onions, chopped

3 medium carrots, peeled and diced

3 celery stalks, diced

6 sprigs fresh parsley

2 bay leaves

½ tsp dried thyme

1 whole fresh 3–4-lb salmon, or 3 lbs thick salmon steaks

¼ tsp salt

¼ tsp black pepper

1 cup dry red wine

1½ Tbs margarine

1½ Tbs flour

1 cup yogurt

EQUIPMENT

peeler   chopper   cheesecloth   large baking pan   2-qt saucepan   wire whisk

PREPARATION

Preheat   oven to 325°F.

Spread   onions, carrots, and celery in bottom of baking pan large enough to hold fish.

Cut   6-inch square of cheesecloth.

Combine   parsley, bay leaves, and thyme, and tie mixture in cheesecloth square and place in baking pan.

Lay   salmon on top of vegetables; sprinkle with salt and pepper and add wine.

Bake   40 to 50 minutes for whole salmon, 30 to 40 minutes for salmon steaks, or until fish flakes easily.

Lower   oven to 200°F to keep fish warm.

Strain   liquid from baking dish; discard all solids.

Melt   margarine in saucepan over low heat; stir flour into margarine with wire whisk.

Add   strained liquid very slowly, stirring constantly with whisk until mixture thickens and comes to a boil; then remove from heat and slowly add yogurt, while continuing to stir.

The sauce may be served over the fish or on the side.

LUXEMBOURG   **CRAYFISH WITH
CARROTS**

SERVINGS: 6–9

TIME NEEDED: 30 minutes, plus simmering and boiling time

INGREDIENTS

3 Tbs margarine

1 carrot, peeled and cut into
   julienne strips

2 medium onions, thinly sliced

1 shallot, chopped

2 cups water

¼ tsp freshly ground black
   pepper

⅛ tsp cayenne pepper

¼ tsp salt

6 sprigs fresh parsley

¼ tsp dried chervil

1 bay leaf

4 cups dry white wine

18 crayfish or 36 large shrimp,
   shelled and cleaned

2 Tbs chopped fresh parsley

EQUIPMENT

peeler   chopper   3-qt Dutch oven   pepper mill   medium bowl
slotted spoon

PREPARATION

Melt   2 Tbs margarine in Dutch oven over moderate heat.

Add   carrots, onions, and shallot.

Cook   until tender.

Add   water, black pepper, cayenne pepper, salt, parsley sprigs, chervil, bay leaf, and wine.

Bring   to a boil and then reduce heat to low.

Simmer   10 minutes.

Add   crayfish or shrimp.

Cook   4 to 5 minutes, or until shellfish turn pink and tails curl up; take Dutch oven from heat, and with slotted spoon remove shellfish to bowl.

Return   Dutch oven to heat and boil liquid over moderate heat until it is reduced to about 2 cups.

Return   shellfish to liquid and rewarm 5 minutes on low to medium heat.

Remove   cooked sprigs of parsley from sauce and add chopped parsley plus 1 Tb margarine; stir well.

Serve   hot.

MYANMAR (BURMA)   **SHRIMP AND ONION CURRY**

SERVINGS: 2–3

TIME NEEDED: About 20 minutes, plus marinating time

INGREDIENTS

12 medium shrimp, shelled and deveined

½ tsp turmeric

1 tsp paprika

½ tsp shrimp sauce or fish soy sauce (optional)*

2 Tbs vegetable oil

3 cups minced onion

3 garlic cloves, minced

½ tsp ground ginger

1 cup water

1 cup tomato puree

EQUIPMENT

medium bowl   medium skillet

PREPARATION

Combine   shrimp in bowl with turmeric and paprika, and shrimp sauce or fish soy sauce if desired.

Marinate   1 hour.

Heat   oil in skillet.

Sauté   onions and garlic in skillet.

Add   ginger.

Simmer   2 minutes.

Add   shrimp mixture to onion mixture.

Stir   occasionally until all shrimp begin to turn pink evenly (2 to 3 minutes).

Stir   water into tomato puree.

Add   puree to shrimp mixture.

Cook   over low heat until sauce and oil appear to separate.

Serve   over hot rice.

*Shrimp sauce has the consistency of a paste. Like fish soy sauce, it is usually available at Asiatic import shops or specialty food shops. Be cautious in using either: both sauces have a very strong flavor.

NEW ZEALAND   **BAKED TROUT**

SERVINGS: 6–8 (depending on size of fish)
TIME NEEDED: 15 minutes, plus baking time

INGREDIENTS

½ tsp salt
1 tsp black pepper
6 small rainbow trout

2 Tbs margarine
60 sprigs fresh mint, chopped

EQUIPMENT

large shallow baking pan   aluminum foil

PREPARATION

Preheat oven to 350°F.
Mix salt and pepper.
Sprinkle inside of each trout with one-sixth of the seasoning mixture.
Dot 1 tsp margarine and one-sixth portion of chopped mint inside each trout.
Wrap each trout in separate piece of foil.
Place wrapped fish side by side in baking pan.
Bake 15 minutes, or until fish flakes easily when tested.
Serve hot.

If some of the cooked fish is to be stored, keep it in its own foil in the refrigerator or freezer. Fish from the refrigerator (or after thawing) may be reheated in its foil in the oven at 350°F for about 10 minutes.

TRINIDAD AND TOBAGO **BAKED FISH**

SERVINGS: 6–8
TIME NEEDED: 15 minutes, plus baking time

INGREDIENTS

⅛ tsp salt
¼ tsp black pepper
4 lbs firm fish (sea trout, kingfish, sea bass)

2 Tbs flour
3–6 thin lean bacon strips (optional)*

EQUIPMENT

large shallow oiled or nonstick baking pan

PREPARATION

Preheat oven to 350°F.
Combine salt and pepper, and sprinkle mixture over both sides of fish. Dust evenly with flour.
Arrange fish in center of pan. If fish has been cut into portions, make sure the pieces do not overlap in pan.
Bake 30 to 40 minutes, or until fish flakes easily with a fork.
Serve hot.

This recipe is customarily served with Creole Sauce (page 56).

*If bacon is permitted in your diet, cover the fish with the bacon strips; you may want to use a substitute such as turkey bacon. The baking time then needs to be increased by about 10 minutes for the bacon to be crisp and the fish to be done.

ALBANIA CHICKEN WITH WALNUT SAUCE

SERVINGS: 6

TIME NEEDED: 40 minutes, plus baking, simmering, and standing time

INGREDIENTS

½ tsp black pepper	1 cup shelled walnuts*
⅛ tsp salt	3 Tbs margarine
1 4–5-lb stewing chicken	2 Tbs flour
3 cups water	1 small garlic clove, minced

EQUIPMENT

large baking dish with cover   rolling pin, blender, or processor
12-inch skillet

PREPARATION

Preheat	oven to 325°F.
Combine	pepper and salt; season chicken by rubbing with pepper-salt mixture.
Place	chicken in baking dish; then add water.
Bake	2 hours, covered, or until chicken is tender.
Crush	walnuts with rolling pin, blender, or processor.
Melt	margarine in skillet over low heat; add flour gradually, and stir well to keep lumps from forming, until flour is brown.
Add	crushed walnuts and garlic.
Cut	cooked chicken into serving pieces, and set aside; reserve broth and skim fat from it.
Add	broth gradually to walnut mixture, stirring well to blend all ingredients thoroughly.
Place	chicken pieces in skillet, and cover each with sauce.
Simmer	over low heat until sauce thickens; then cover pan and remove from heat.
Let stand	5 to 10 minutes before serving to allow flavors to blend fully.

*If nuts are to be avoided (because of their fat content), the chicken can be removed from the skillet a few minutes before serving to allow the sauce to drain off.

BARBADOS # CHICKEN-DOWN-IN-RICE

SERVINGS: 6

TIME NEEDED: 25 minutes, plus standing and simmering time

INGREDIENTS

1 4-lb chicken
1 Tb lime juice
¼ tsp salt
2 qts water
4 cups uncooked long-grain
  rice

¼ tsp dried thyme
¼ tsp dried savory
¼ tsp dried marjoram
¼ tsp black pepper

EQUIPMENT

7-qt Dutch oven   large serving platter

PREPARATION

Rub   chicken with lime juice and salt.
Set   aside for 30 minutes.
Pour   water over seasoned chicken in Dutch oven.
Bring   to a boil over moderate heat; then reduce to low heat.
Simmer 30 minutes, covered.
Add   rice, thyme, savory, marjoram, and pepper.
Simmer 40 minutes, covered, or until rice is cooked and chicken is
        tender.
Carve   chicken into serving-size pieces.
Serve   by arranging portions around a mound of cooked rice in the
        center of a large platter.

This dish usually appears with a sauce (often of giblets) poured on the chicken and/or served on the side. The mushroom sauce on page 51 goes well with this dish.

BOLIVIA   **PICKLED CHICKEN**

SERVINGS: 4–6
TIME NEEDED: 15 minutes, plus simmering and chilling time

INGREDIENTS

1 4-lb stewing chicken, cut into
  serving portions
2 large onions, quartered
3 carrots, cut lengthwise into
  sticks
½ large green pepper, sliced
  into rings

¼ cup olive oil
1 cup wine vinegar
⅓ cup water
⅛ tsp salt
¼ tsp black pepper
1 bay leaf
pinch of allspice

EQUIPMENT

large Dutch oven or stewpot   medium bowl

PREPARATION

Combine   all ingredients in Dutch oven.
  Simmer   1 hour, or until chicken is tender.
  Transfer   chicken with marinade to bowl; skim off any fat that rises
           to the top.
    Chill   thoroughly, preferably overnight.
    Serve   cold.

ETHIOPIA # WAT (STEWED CHICKEN)

SERVINGS: 6–8
TIME NEEDED: 45 minutes, plus simmering time

INGREDIENTS

2 Tbs olive oil
2 cups finely chopped shallots
2 3½-lb chickens, cut into
    serving portions
1½ Tbs cayenne pepper*
2 tsps ground ginger
1½ tsps ground cumin
¾ tsp ground cardamom

1 tsp ground cinnamon
½ tsp black pepper
¼ tsp salt
¼ tsp ground nutmeg
⅛ tsp turmeric
½ tsp ground cloves
3½ cups water

EQUIPMENT

chopper   7-qt Dutch oven or clay pot   medium bowl

PREPARATION

Heat oil in Dutch oven over moderate heat and cook shallots until golden; set aside in bowl.

Brown chicken pieces, a few at a time, 5 to 10 minutes, turning them on all sides until lightly browned, then setting aside with shallots.

Combine seasonings with chicken and shallots in Dutch oven, and mix well.

Add water and heat mixture to boiling; then lower heat.

Simmer 1 hour, covered, or until chicken reaches desired tenderness.

Serve hot.

A literal translation from the original Ethiopian recipe reads: "Kill the chicken and prepare it for cooking. Put the chopped red shallots in the clay pot and stir them well until they are golden brown."

*Traditionally this dish is very "hot." For a milder version, decrease the amount of cayenne and/or black pepper to desired taste.

KOREA   **SPICY CHICKEN**

SERVINGS: 6–8
TIME NEEDED: 35 minutes, plus baking time

INGREDIENTS

2 3½-lb chickens
6 garlic cloves, minced
2 medium onions, very finely
  chopped
½ tsp crushed red pepper
½ tsp ground cloves
¼ tsp salt

¼ tsp ground cardamom
1 tsp ground ginger
½ cup finely ground almonds
3 Tbs vegetable oil
2½ tsps freshly ground black
  pepper

EQUIPMENT

small bowl   chopper   grinder or processor   large greased or
nonstick roasting pan   spatula

PREPARATION

Preheat   oven to 350°F.
Remove   and discard skin from chickens, except for wings.
Prick   chicken flesh all over with a fork.
Combine   garlic and onions in bowl with rest of ingredients.
Blend   seasonings thoroughly to form a paste.
Rub   seasoning paste over entire exterior surface of chickens, and rub a little inside as well.
Bake   chickens in roasting pan 1½ hours, or until chicken is golden-brown and tender.

SENEGAL ## LEMON CHICKEN

SERVINGS: 6–8

TIME NEEDED: 40 minutes, plus marinating and simmering time

INGREDIENTS

2 3-lb chickens
3 medium onions, chopped
½ cup fresh lemon juice
½ tsp cayenne pepper

¼ tsp salt
2 Tbs vegetable oil
½ cup water

EQUIPMENT

large bowl or pot   chopper   juicer   paper towels   sieve
7-qt Dutch oven

PREPARATION

Wash chickens, cut into serving-size pieces, and place in large bowl.

Sprinkle onions on chicken, and then fresh lemon juice, cayenne pepper, and salt.

Toss pieces to coat evenly with seasoning.

Refrigerate 12 hours minimum, covered; it is best to keep in marinade up to 48 hours, turning pieces over occasionally to distribute liquid evenly.

Remove chicken from marinade and dry pieces on paper towels.

Strain marinade and set onions and liquid aside separately.

Heat oil in Dutch oven on moderately high heat.

Add chicken pieces and sear until brown all over; remove and set aside.

Brown onions lightly in Dutch oven.

Add chicken pieces, water, and strained marinade liquid.

Simmer 40 minutes, covered, on low heat, or until chicken is tender.

Serve hot.

UNITED STATES   **COUNTRY INN CHICKEN**

SERVINGS: 2
TIME NEEDED: 15 minutes, plus baking time

INGREDIENTS

2 Tbs flour
1 tsp grated lemon peel
¼ tsp paprika
¼ tsp dried rosemary
⅛ tsp salt
¼ tsp freshly ground black pepper

2 large chicken breast halves
2 Tbs vegetable oil
¼ cup water
¼ cup dry white wine

EQUIPMENT

medium paper bag   grater   10-inch skillet   2-qt casserole
heated platter

PREPARATION

Preheat   oven to 350°F.

Combine   flour, lemon peel, paprika, rosemary, salt, and pepper in paper bag.

Add   chicken and shake bag well to coat pieces with seasonings.

Heat   oil in skillet over moderate heat.

Add   chicken and brown evenly on both sides.

Remove   chicken to casserole, and add water and wine.

Bake   20 minutes, covered; then 15 minutes, uncovered, or until tender.

Remove   chicken to heated platter and keep warm until serving, preferably with a sauce such as Country Inn Sauce (page 57).

ZAMBIA **SIMMERED CHICKEN**

SERVINGS: 4–6
TIME NEEDED: 45 minutes, plus simmering and cooling time

INGREDIENTS

1 4–5-lb chicken
¼ tsp salt
½ tsp pepper
2 Tbs vegetable oil
2 large onions, diced or
   coarsely chopped

4 large fresh or canned
   tomatoes, sliced
1½ cups chicken broth,
   skimmed

EQUIPMENT

6-qt Dutch oven   chopper   paper towels   large bowl

PREPARATION

Wash   chicken and cut into serving-size pieces.
Rub   salt and pepper over chicken.
Let   pieces rest for 20 minutes.
Heat   oil in Dutch oven.
Braise   each piece of chicken in hot oil until golden on both sides; set on paper towels to drain.
Sauté   onions until limp and just beginning to brown; then add tomatoes and lower heat.
Simmer   5 minutes.
Add   chicken pieces and chicken broth, and stir well.
Simmer   1¼ hours, uncovered, turning chicken pieces over occasionally until all are tender.
Remove   chicken to bowl and let gravy cool in Dutch oven until fat has risen to the top; skim fat off.
Replace   chicken in Dutch oven and reheat.

This dish is traditionally served with rice, mashed potatoes, or cooked cornmeal.

AFGHANISTAN ## LAMB AND RICE

SERVINGS: 6–8
TIME NEEDED: 35 minutes, plus simmering and baking time

INGREDIENTS

6 lean lamb shanks
¼ tsp salt
1 medium onion, diced
water
2 Tbs vegetable oil*

1 tsp ground cumin
1¾ cups uncooked long-grain rice
oil for greasing

EQUIPMENT

3-qt saucepan   large skillet   paper towels   holding platter
10 × 14-inch baking dish

PREPARATION

Combine lamb, salt, and half of diced onion in saucepan with enough water to cover meat.

Simmer 1½ hours, covered, or until meat is tender.

Remove lamb from broth; reserve broth.

Preheat oven to 450°F.

Heat oil in skillet (or use nonstick skillet without oil) and add lamb, turning until well browned; remove lamb from skillet and drain well on paper towels.

Brown remaining onion in skillet; reserve onions, but drain fat.

Skim fat from broth in which lamb was cooked; to 3½–4 cups broth in saucepan add browned onion, cumin, and rice.

Simmer 20 minutes, covered, or until broth is absorbed and rice is tender.

Place browned lamb shanks in oiled baking dish, and cover meat with cooked rice.

Bake 30 minutes.

Serve immediately, while hot.

*If you wish to limit the amount of fat, use a nonstick skillet without oil for the browning.

GABON   # LAMB STEW

SERVINGS: 8
TIME NEEDED: 30 minutes, plus simmering time

INGREDIENTS

2 Tbs vegetable oil   *1 cup thin beef broth*
3 lbs lean, trimmed, boneless   *1 cup medium-dry red wine*
*   lamb, cut into 2-inch cubes**   *1/4 tsp black pepper*
2 medium onions, chopped   *1/8 tsp cayenne pepper*
2 green peppers, seeded and   *1/8 tsp Tabasco sauce*
*   chopped*   *1/8 tsp salt*
1 1-lb can tomatoes   *1/2 cup sliced fresh mushrooms*
1/2 cup tomato puree

EQUIPMENT

4-qt Dutch oven   slotted spoon

PREPARATION

Heat   oil in Dutch oven.

Braise   lamb cubes in batches, browning them on all sides; set aside.

Cook   onions and green peppers in Dutch oven until tender.

Add   reserved lamb cubes, tomatoes, tomato puree, beef broth, wine, black pepper, cayenne pepper, Tabasco sauce, and salt.

Bring   to a boil over moderate heat; then lower heat.

Simmer   1 hour, covered; add mushrooms.

Simmer   30 minutes, or until meat is tender.

Remove   meat with slotted spoon to drain as much fat off as possible, and serve promptly.

*Instead of lamb, a 3-lb fowl can be substituted; the first simmering time should then be cut to 30 minutes.

GUYANA   # GARLIC PORK

SERVINGS: 6–8 (as entrée); 12–18 (as hors d'oeuvres)
TIME NEEDED: 50 minutes, plus marinating time

INGREDIENTS

2 lbs very lean, trimmed,   1 Tb dried thyme
  boneless pork   ⅛ tsp salt
1¼ cups white vinegar   ½ tsp cayenne pepper
1¼ cups water   vegetable oil (for coating skillet
10 large garlic cloves   or wok)

EQUIPMENT

medium bowl   colander or sieve   mortar or processor   vegetable
oil   paper towels   large heavy skillet or wok   ovenproof platter

PREPARATION

Cut	pork into small cubes, 1-inch for entrée, ½ inch cubes for hours d'oeuvres.
Combine	¼ cup vinegar and ¼ cup water in bowl.
Add	pork cubes and stir well to cover pieces.
Drain	liquid from pork; rinse meat under cold water and return to bowl.
Crush	large garlic cloves and place in mortar or processor; add thyme, salt, and cayenne pepper.
Grind	seasonings in mortar until smooth paste forms.
Add	paste and remaining water and vinegar to pork.
Stir	meat and marinade well, making sure each cube is covered with seasonings. If there is not enough liquid to cover meat, add small, equal amounts of vinegar and water.
Refrigerate	2 to 3 days, covered, stirring from time to time to marinate pork thoroughly; then remove cubes from marinade and dry on paper towels.
Preheat	oven to 200°F.
Heat	skillet or wok until hot; if using nonstick skillet or wok, coat with small amount of oil.
Braise	pork cubes, several at a time, for about 2 to 3 minutes each; smaller cubes may need only 1 to 2 minutes for browning.
Drain	cubes on paper towels on platter in warming oven.

MALI # LAMB WITH EGGPLANT

SERVINGS: 6

TIME NEEDED: 55 minutes, plus simmering time

INGREDIENTS

2 Tbs vegetable oil
3 lbs trimmed lamb neck bones
4 scallions, chopped
1 tomato, chopped
1 Tb tomato paste
1 green pepper, seeded and
  chopped

1 medium eggplant, peeled
  and diced
1 qt water
½ tsp black pepper
¼ tsp salt
4 Tbs peanut butter
3–4 cups cooked rice

EQUIPMENT

7-qt Dutch oven   chopper

PREPARATION

Heat   vegetable oil in Dutch oven.

Braise   lamb neck bones, browning on all sides; remove from Dutch oven and set aside.

Cook   scallions in Dutch oven, stirring occasionally.

Add   tomato, tomato paste, green pepper, and eggplant.

Cook   5 minutes, stirring occasionally.

Add   browned meat, water, black pepper, and salt.

Bring   to a boil; then lower heat.

Simmer   1½ hours, covered, or until meat is tender.

Add   peanut butter gradually; blend well.

Simmer   5 minutes, or until liquid thickens slightly.

Serve   hot over mound of hot rice.

SAUDI ARABIA   ROAST LAMB

SERVINGS: 8–10

TIME NEEDED: 25 minutes, plus roasting time

INGREDIENTS

1 leg of lamb (about 4 lbs), trimmed, with bone removed	2 medium onions, chopped
¼ tsp salt	1 Tb margarine
¼ tsp black pepper	1 Tb vegetable oil
	½ cup water

EQUIPMENT

chopper   large roasting pan   string

PREPARATION

Preheat   oven to 325°F.

Wash   and dry leg of lamb.

Mix   salt with pepper and sprinkle mixture in meat cavity left by removal of bone.

Stuff   onions inside cavity and dot with tiny bits of margarine.

Roll   leg of lamb up so both ends are tucked inside to form a neat roll; tie both ends securely with string.

Rub   outside of lamb roll with oil.

Pour   water into roasting pan.

Roast   lamb about 1¾ hours (longer if lamb is desired very well done). Baste occasionally with water from pan; if pan dries out, add more water, a little at a time, as needed.

Serve   hot or cold, sliced thinly.

SOUTH AFRICA **TOMATO BREDIE**

SERVINGS: 6

TIME NEEDED: 35 minutes, plus simmering time

INGREDIENTS

2 Tbs vegetable oil

6 shoulder lamb chops,
   trimmed

2 large onions, sliced

3 lbs ripe tomatoes, peeled and
   chopped

1 tsp ground cinnamon

1 bay leaf

⅛ tsp salt

¼ tsp black pepper

pinch or two of brown sugar
   (optional)

EQUIPMENT

4-qt Dutch oven   chopper

PREPARATION

Heat oil in Dutch oven over moderate heat.

Add lamb chops and braise until brown on both sides; then remove from pan and set aside.

Cook onions in Dutch oven, stirring a little until golden.

Add tomatoes, cinnamon, bay leaf, salt, and pepper to cooked onions.

Cook over moderate heat until mixture thickens; stir from time to time to keep from sticking or burning.*

Layer browned lamb chops over sauce.

Simmer 1¼ to 1½ hours, covered, over low heat, or until chops are tender.

*Taste sauce at this point to see if it is too acidic instead of slightly sweet. If tomatoes were not fully sun-ripened, they may not be sweet enough; a pinch or two of brown sugar may correct the taste.

THAILAND   **SWEET-AND-SOUR PORK**

SERVINGS: 6
TIME NEEDED: 45 minutes

INGREDIENTS

1 Tb vegetable oil
1½ lbs lean, trimmed, boneless
  pork, thinly sliced
1½ large cucumbers
1 large onion, sliced
1 garlic clove, minced
4 2-inch green chili peppers,
  seeded and sliced into very
  thin strips

4 medium tomatoes, each cut
  into 8 pieces
2 Tbs sugar
2 Tbs white vinegar
1 Tb soy sauce
½ cup chicken stock, skimmed

EQUIPMENT

large heavy skillet or wok   meat slicer or electric knife   large
platter

PREPARATION

Heat   oil in skillet (if not nonstick variety); heat only ½ Tb oil if
       using wok.

Add   pork slices a few at a time to skillet; stir occasionally until
       all are lightly browned and cooked. Then remove and re-
       serve on platter.

Peel   cucumbers; cut in half across, then lengthwise into quar-
       ters.

Reheat   skillet; add a little oil, if necessary.

Cook   cucumbers in skillet, browning lightly but keeping them
       crisp; then remove to platter.

Sauté   onion slices in skillet until tender and lightly brown; then
       remove to platter.

Cook   garlic and pepper strips in skillet over moderate heat until
       tender; add tomatoes. Brown entire mixture quickly.

Add   sugar, vinegar, soy sauce, and chicken stock.

Heat   to boiling and add all reserved ingredients from platter.

Stir   well and heat thoroughly.

THE UKRAINE **PORK AND MUSHROOM CASSEROLE**

SERVINGS: 6
TIME NEEDED: 55 minutes, plus baking time

INGREDIENTS

2 Tbs margarine
½ lb mushrooms, sliced
1 medium onion, chopped
1 Tb flour
⅛ tsp salt
⅛ tsp black pepper

1½ lbs lean, trimmed, boneless
   pork, sliced into very thin
   strips
½ cup yogurt
½ cup water
¼ cup chopped fresh parsley

EQUIPMENT

10-inch skillet   chopper   2 small bowls   3-qt Dutch oven

PREPARATION

Preheat   oven to 350°F.

Melt   margarine in skillet over moderate heat.

Sauté   mushrooms and onion in skillet until lightly browned; then set aside.

Combine   flour, salt, and pepper in bowl.

Toss   pork strips in flour mixture; coat very lightly.

Braise   pork strips a few at a time in skillet over moderate heat until lightly browned; then set aside.

Arrange   half the meat slices on bottom of Dutch oven and cover with half the mushroom-onion mixture.

Layer   rest of meat slices and mushroom-onion mixture.

Mix   yogurt in small bowl with water and pour over meat.

Bake   45 minutes, covered.

Serve   hot, garnished with parsley.

GERMANY **MERINGUE TORTE**

SERVINGS: 8
TIME NEEDED: 30 minutes, plus slow baking time

INGREDIENTS

4 egg whites	1 cup sugar
¼ tsp salt	¼ tsp vanilla extract*
¼ tsp cream of tartar	

EQUIPMENT

8-inch springform baking pan (coat lightly with nonstick spray, or use nonstick pan)† whisk or beater large bowl narrow spatula

PREPARATION

Preheat oven to 450°F.

Beat egg whites and salt until very foamy.

Add cream of tartar and beat until soft, firm peaks form; then add sugar gradually, beating until sugar dissolves and whites form stiff peaks that hold their shape.

Blend vanilla lightly into egg whites.

Fill springform with meringue, using spatula to spread evenly; then place pan in center of oven.

Turn oven off *immediately*, leaving oven door closed.

Leave meringue in oven overnight, or at least 5 to 6 hours so it can bake slowly as heat in the oven gradually dissipates.

Serve cold with fresh or stewed fruit, chopped nuts, cottage cheese with raisins, or any similar favorite filling in the center.

*Almond extract or anisette flavoring may be substituted for vanilla.
†If a springform is not available, make this torte the old-fashioned way: Line a baking sheet with a large sheet of heavy brown paper, such as a shopping bag. Put an 8-inch plate in the center and outline it on the paper. Remove the plate and set a glass about 3 inches in diameter in the middle of the circle. Spread a layer of meringue (at least ½ inch thick) in a circle around the glass. Spread the rest of the meringue around the edges of that circle with spatula to pile it up.

PEACHES POACHED IN WINE

SERVINGS: 12
TIME NEEDED: 20 minutes, plus simmering and chilling time

INGREDIENTS

12 large, firm, ripe peaches,
pitted and cut in halves
1½ cups sweet light wine
(rosé, muscatel, Sauternes,
or port)

½ cup sugar
⅔ cup water
rum (optional)

EQUIPMENT

very large skillet or Dutch oven or sauté pan   small bowl   slotted spatula or spoon   large bowl

PREPARATION

Place peach halves in single layer in pan, overlapping as little as possible.

Mix wine in small bowl with sugar and water; pour over peaches.

Simmer 5 to 10 minutes over very low heat, or until peaches are tender but still firm.

Transfer peaches to large bowl using spatula and being careful not to break them into pieces.

Pour hot wine syrup over fruit.

Chill thoroughly in refrigerator.

Serve very cold.

In some parts of Italy, a few spoonfuls of rum are poured over chilled peaches just before serving.

MEXICO   # BREAD PUDDING

SERVINGS: 8
TIME NEEDED: 30 minutes, plus baking time

INGREDIENTS

8 Tbs margarine	1 tsp ground cinnamon
12 slices day-old bread	½ cup cottage cheese*
1 cup water	½ cup pine nuts
2 cups light brown sugar	

EQUIPMENT

small saucepan   pastry brush   9 × 9 × 2-inch baking pan or large
casserole or loaf pan

PREPARATION

Melt	6 Tbs margarine in saucepan and brush lightly on both sides of bread slices.
Boil	water plus brown sugar and cinnamon, stirring until mixture becomes quite syrupy; then remove from heat.
Preheat	oven to 350°F.
Coat	baking pan with very light layer margarine; place one layer of bread in pan.
Spread	some cottage cheese and pine nuts onto layer of bread.
Pour	part of warm syrup onto bread-cheese-nut mixture; add a few tiny dots margarine.
Layer	remaining bread and other ingredients.
Bake	20 minutes, or until top is golden brown.
Serve	hot with whipped or fresh-fruit topping, or fresh berry sauce.

*Various brands of reduced-cholesterol, reduced-fat cottage cheese are now
generally available.

PORTUGAL ### BANANA SOUFFLÉ

SERVINGS: 3 to 4
TIME NEEDED: 15 minutes, plus baking time

INGREDIENTS

4 bananas   4 egg whites
2 Tbs sugar   ½ tsp vanilla extract
2 jiggers or 3 ozs dry red wine
   (traditionally port)

EQUIPMENT

medium baking dish   medium bowl   beater

PREPARATION

Slice   3 bananas very thin and arrange in bottom of baking dish.
Sprinkle   1 Tb sugar over bananas.
Pour   wine over bananas.
Stir   1 Tb sugar and vanilla extract into egg whites.
Beat   egg whites until firm but not dry.
Spread   beaten whites on bananas as topping.
Bake   about 20 minutes, or until meringue just begins to brown.
Slice   remaining banana very thin and spread as decoration atop soufflé before serving.

SWEDEN   **BAKED PEARS**

SERVINGS: 2
TIME NEEDED: 10 minutes, plus baking time

INGREDIENTS

3 Tbs sugar
¾ tsp curry powder
1½ tsps cornstarch
⅛ tsp salt
½ cup unsweetened pineapple
  juice

2 tsps lemon juice
2 firm fresh pears, or 4 canned
  pear halves
1 Tb melted unsalted
  margarine

EQUIPMENT

1-qt saucepan   parer/corer   1½-qt shallow baking dish

PREPARATION

Preheat oven to 350°F.
Combine sugar, curry powder, cornstarch, and salt in saucepan.
   Stir pineapple juice into mixture, blending well until smooth;
     then stir in lemon juice; cook over moderate heat, stirring
     constantly until sauce thickens and comes to a boil; then
     remove from heat.
   Pare fresh pears; then core and cut in half.
Arrange pear halves in baking dish with cored centers up.
   Pour sauce and melted margarine over pears.
   Bake 20 to 30 minutes until fresh pears are tender. (Canned
     pears need less cooking time and should be removed as
     soon as heated through.)
  Serve pears with sauce immediately.

Curry flavor tends to get stronger after standing. Do not pour sauce
over pears and bake until near mealtime so they can be served
promptly. If cut pears are to stand for a while before sauce is poured
over them, sprinkle with lemon juice or a fresh-fruit preservative to
keep them from turning brown.

UNITED STATES ## BUCCANEER NUGGET CAKE

YIELD: 15 3-inch squares
TIME NEEDED: 25 minutes, plus baking time

INGREDIENTS

5 egg whites	½ lb dates, chopped
½ cup sugar	½ tsp vanilla extract
1 cup chopped pecans	1 tsp baking powder
1 cup unsalted cracker crumbs	⅛ tsp salt

EQUIPMENT

chopper   beater   medium mixing bowl   10 × 15 × 1½-inch
jelly-roll pan, greased or nonstick

PREPARATION

Preheat   oven to 300°F.
Beat   egg whites in bowl until frothy.
Add   sugar gradually, 1 spoonful at a time; beat until stiff peaks form.
Fold   pecans into egg mixture.
Fold   cracker crumbs into mixture.
Add   all but 2 Tbs dates plus vanilla extract, baking powder, and salt.
Spread   batter evenly in jelly-roll pan.
Sprinkle   remaining 2 Tbs dates over top.
Bake   25 to 30 minutes, or until lightly brown and firm.
Cut   into 3-inch squares when completely cooled.

UNITED STATES   **GRAHAM-CRACKER
PIE CRUST**

YIELD: 6–8 portions for pie
TIME NEEDED: 10 minutes, plus baking time

INGREDIENTS

¼ cup margarine
¼ cup confectioners' sugar,
  sifted

1⅓ cups graham cracker
  crumbs*

EQUIPMENT

rolling pin or processor   sifter   medium bowl   9-inch pie pan

PREPARATION

Preheat oven to 375°F.
   Melt margarine; add margarine and sugar to graham cracker
         crumbs.
  Blend mixture well and press firmly and evenly into pie pan.
   Bake 5 minutes; then let cool before adding pie filling and final
         baking.

Some recipes call for filling graham cracker crust immediately, without baking it first.

*About twelve graham crackers are needed. The crackers can be crushed with a rolling pin or crumbled finely in a processor.

UNITED STATES   ## NUT CRISPS

YIELD: 4 dozen cookies
TIME NEEDED: 40 minutes, plus baking time

INGREDIENTS

½ lb soft unsalted margarine	pinch of salt
½ cup confectioners' sugar	2 cups chopped toasted
2 cups sifted flour	almonds*
2 tsps vanilla extract	confectioners' sugar for dusting

EQUIPMENT

medium bowl   beater   cookie sheets, nonstick or greased
wire cooking rack   wide spatula   jelly-roll pan or cookie sheet

PREPARATION

Preheat   oven to 350°F.

Beat   margarine in bowl until smooth and creamy.

Add   confectioners' sugar gradually, beating until fluffy; then add flour, vanilla extract, and salt.

Blend   ingredients thoroughly; add almonds to batter, stirring lightly.

Shape   cake mixture with floured hands into "logs," about 1½ inches long and ½ inch thick.

Place   logs about 1½ inches apart on cookie sheets.

Bake   10 to 15 minutes, or until light golden brown.

Remove   carefully with wide spatula onto wire racks to cool.

Sprinkle   lightly with confectioners' sugar.

*To toast almonds, spread them in single layer in jelly-roll pan. Bake in preheated 350°F oven; stir occasionally until very lightly browned, about 10 minutes.

YEMEN   # DATE-FILLED COOKIES

SERVINGS: 12
TIME NEEDED: 45 minutes, plus refrigerating and baking time

INGREDIENTS

2 cups sifted flour
½ tsp baking powder
¼ tsp salt
½ cup margarine, softened

¼ cup milk
2 Tbs margarine
1 cup pitted dates, cut into
   halves

EQUIPMENT

sifter   2 large bowls   wooden spoon or beater   wax paper
pastry brush   pastry board   very small saucepan or skillet
rolling pin   baking sheet, ungreased

PREPARATION

Combine   flour, baking powder, and salt; sift into bowl.
   Cream   softened margarine in second bowl with wooden spoon or
            beater until smooth.
     Add   flour mixture to margarine, alternating with portions of
            milk; beat until well blended and dough holds its shape.
    Mold   dough into roll about 2½ inches in diameter; then wrap
            in wax paper and chill 30 minutes in refrigerator.
 Preheat   oven to 375°F.
    Melt   2 Tbs margarine in skillet and brush over dates.
     Cut   cold dough into ¼-inch slices; then roll each slice out until
            it forms 4-inch round.
     Set   3 or 4 date halves into center of each round; moisten
            edges of dough with water; fold cookie round in half to
            form half moon.
    Seal   edges of dough by pressing down with fork tongs.
    Bake   20 to 25 minutes on baking sheet, or until golden brown.

Reduced Fat Recipes

INTRODUCTION

At no other time in the history of this country have so many people been so health conscious and so desperate to keep from gaining too much weight.

At the same time, it gets harder and harder to resist the endless spectrum of enticing between-meal snacks, from niblets of fried chicken, breaded shrimp, or bacon-wrapped meatballs, to ice cream, buttery cakes, and chocolate chip cookies. Yet those snacks quickly add on calories and increase our fat intake to a surprising extent. For instance, one slice (about 1 ounce) of any of the well-known brands of bologna contains as much as 6–9 grams of fat. Fat content in a 5-ounce cup of yogurt can run from as little as 1 gram, up to as much as 4 grams, depending on the variety and whether it is made from whole or skimmed milk. And just 1 ounce of a chocolate bar with almonds can add another 10 grams to the fat burden.

Given this scenario, it's scarcely surprising that up to as much as 50 percent of the calories consumed by a great many Americans is in the form of fat. For years after World War II, consumption of fats and oils steadily increased. Luckily, as health professionals became increasingly aware of the problems this caused and spoke out, their message began to reach the public: *Fat poses a double danger*. Its high caloric content can quickly add on those unwanted pounds, and its cholesterol content can imperil our arteries.

However, a totally fat-free diet can also prove to be harmful. We need some fat in our foods. It's a prime source of energy that's released more slowly than the "quick pickup" we get from carbohydrates. It also supplies some essential fatty acids that our own organs cannot manufacture, as well as providing a natural storehouse of fat-soluble vitamins (A, D, E, and K). Nonetheless, there remain two key questions: how much fat should we consume, and what kind?

The amount and type of fat we eat are critical factors in helping to keep our arteries in good shape. Large amounts of certain fatty foods, such as "marbled" steak, eggs, or pie crusts made with lard, raise cholesterol levels. That, as we noted in part I, can mean a greater risk of coronary heart disease. On the other hand, using the favorable kinds of polyunsaturated fat, like safflower and sunflower oils, can help lower serum cholesterol levels.

In simplest terms, fats fall into three types. Saturated fats are the bugaboo. They are the kind your body tends to turn into cholesterol. Unfortunately, it's saturated fat that's present in some of the most popular traditional foods throughout the world. These are beef, pork, butter, whole milk, and cocoa butter (chocolate), as well as a few vegetable sources, such as coconut and palm oil. In general, organ meats such as liver and brains, whether from beef or pork, are particularly high in saturated fat and should be used sparingly even in the normal diet.

The other types of fat, mono- and polyunsaturated, pose less of a health risk. The monounsaturated type is present in virtually all foods of animal origin and in a few vegetable products as well. This kind can help reduce the level of certain forms of cholesterol. For example, oleic acid, the chief monounsaturated oil from olives, has been shown to reduce certain forms of cholesterol by up to as much as 15 percent. Oils from peanuts and avocados are also monounsaturated. Linoleic acid, the major constituent in polyunsaturated fats, is present in corn, soy, cottonseed, safflower, and sunflower oils. It, too, has been shown to lower LDL (low-density lipoprotein) cholesterol by up to 15 percent.

The third variety, the polyunsaturated form, is the most desirable since it is not transformed into cholesterol. This type comes largely from vegetables. Therefore, wherever possible, it's preferable to cook with safflower, sunflower, corn, soybean, and cottonseed oils rather than with butter or hydrogenated products, such as lard or the solid products often used as shortening. Some fish oils are also polyunsaturated. This is why heart patients and those who are obese are often advised to eat more fish rather than red meats.

While it's essential to learn which are the high-fat foods to be avoided or eaten only sparingly, it's equally important to switch to preparation and cooking methods that help you get rid of excess fat in the foods you buy.

The recipes in this section are not offered as a diet plan either for weight reduction for obese patients, or for lowering cholesterol in patients with a high blood lipid (fat) condition. Sharply restricted dietary regimens should not be undertaken without a doctor's advice. However, if you have any such specific medical problem and must be on a restricted diet plan, many of the recipes in this section may meet with your doctor's approval and can provide a way of adding variety to your menus.

Most of all, we hope the international recipes in this section will satisfy both the appetite and the wanderlust of your family and guests by introducing a touch of "foreign" excitement to their meals, yet without adding unnecessary and unwanted fat.

AUSTRALIA
TOMATO PIE

SERVINGS: 4–6
TIME NEEDED: 20 minutes, plus baking time

INGREDIENTS

2 cups bread crumbs, soft but not too fresh
1 small onion, chopped
1 Tb chopped fresh parsley
1 tsp chopped fresh thyme
½ tsp chopped fresh marjoram

juice of 1 lemon
⅛ tsp salt
¼ tsp black pepper
1½ lbs ripe tomatoes, peeled and thinly sliced
1 tsp margarine

EQUIPMENT

medium bowl   chopper   juicer   ovenproof pie pan

PREPARATION

Preheat oven to 325°F.

Combine bread crumbs, onion, parsley, thyme, marjoram, lemon juice, salt, and pepper in bowl.

Layer tomato slices on bottom of pie plate; cover with seasoned bread crumbs.

Repeat layers until all tomatoes have been used, making sure to end with bread crumb topping.

Dot top of pie with tiny dabs margarine.

Bake about 45 minutes, or until top crust turns light brown.

ISRAEL   # ARTICHOKE FINGERS

SERVINGS: 6
TIME NEEDED: 10 minutes, plus simmering time

INGREDIENTS

1 Tb vegetable oil	¼ tsp hot red-pepper flakes
4 fresh garlic cloves, minced	⅛ tsp salt
12 young tender artichoke	2 cups lukewarm water
stalks	1½ Tbs lemon juice

EQUIPMENT

small skillet   medium shallow saucepan

PREPARATION

Heat   oil in skillet; add garlic and cook until soft and slightly browned.

Peel   artichoke stalks, removing fibers and outer skin.

Wash   stalks in cold water; line them on bottom of medium saucepan.

Add   browned garlic, pepper flakes, salt, and lukewarm water.

Simmer   30 minutes over low heat; then add lemon juice.

Simmer   15 minutes until stalks are tender and most of liquid has evaporated, forming a thick sauce.

Can be served as part of hot buffet, as appetizer, or as side dish with meat.

LESOTHO ## MEALIE BREAD

SERVINGS: 18
TIME NEEDED: 1 hour, plus baking time

INGREDIENTS

3½ cups water
1 tsp salt
2¼ cups white cornmeal

margarine or vegetable oil to
grease skillet

EQUIPMENT

medium saucepan   wooden spoon   pastry board
large heavy skillet   large baking sheets

PREPARATION

Bring water to boil in saucepan with salt; then stir in cornmeal slowly since mixture thickens rapidly.

Remove from heat when cornmeal is completely mixed in; transfer dough to pastry board to cool for 10 minutes.

Knead dough for 15 minutes, with hands dampened in cold water, until dough is smooth and feels almost like satin; then divide it to form balls the size of tennis balls; flatten each one to about 1 inch thick.

Preheat oven to 450°F.

Heat lightly greased skillet and cook bread rounds, several at a time, until light crust forms; then grease skillet again and turn bread over to form crust on other side.

Arrange crusty bread rounds on baking sheets.

Bake 30 minutes, turning each one over every 10 minutes until thick crust forms.

Serve hot, split like English muffins, with favorite spread.

LIBYA   **CHICK PEA DIP**

YIELD: 2 cups
TIME NEEDED: 40 minutes

INGREDIENTS

1 1-lb can chick peas (garbanzo
  beans)
1 garlic clove
¼ tsp salt
4 Tbs tahini (sesame seed
  paste)

4 Tbs lemon juice
dash of paprika
handful of pine nuts
few sprigs fresh parsley, very
  finely chopped

EQUIPMENT

strainer   mill or processor   large bowl   mortar and pestle
chopper

PREPARATION

Strain chick peas and reserve liquid.
Press peas through mill into bowl, or process until very fine.
Combine garlic and salt in mortar; pound into smooth paste. Then
add garlic mixture, chick pea liquid, tahini, and lemon
juice to pureed peas.
Blend thoroughly until very smooth.
Garnish with paprika sprinkled on top, plus pine nuts as border;
toss chopped parsley over center.
Serve at room temperature with unsalted crackers or bits of pita
bread for dipping.

MONGOLIA   **MARINATED BEEF STRIPS**

SERVINGS: 8
TIME NEEDED: 50 minutes, plus marinating time

INGREDIENTS

3 Tbs soy sauce
1 Tb wine vinegar
3 Tbs sugar
2 garlic cloves, minced
½ tsp black pepper

2 green onions, very finely
  chopped
2 lbs very lean round steak, cut
  in narrow 2-inch-long strips

EQUIPMENT

chopper   small bowl   large, shallow pan or platter
slotted pancake turner   paper towels   toothpicks   warming plate
or tray

PREPARATION

Combine   all ingredients except meat in bowl.
Spread   seasonings over beef in pan or platter.
Marinate   1 hour at room temperature; turn meat occasionally, making sure seasoning is spread evenly over strips.
Remove   beef strips with slotted turner; drain on paper towels.
Broil   each strip 3 to 5 minutes each side (check one in first batch to see if done to taste).
Transfer   strips to warming plate or tray.

This dish can be prepared for a hot buffet or as appetizer, with toothpicks inserted for serving individual strips.

UNITED STATES   **WOODBINE RELISH**

YIELD: 6 cups
TIME NEEDED: 40 minutes, plus standing and chilling time

INGREDIENTS

1 large carrot, very finely
  chopped
2 medium onions, chopped
1 medium fresh red pepper,
  seeded and chopped
1 fresh green pepper, seeded
  and chopped
1 medium head green cabbage,
  chopped

½ tsp salt
¾ tsp celery seed
¾ tsp mustard seed
dash of Tabasco sauce
½ cup white vinegar
½ cup sugar

EQUIPMENT

chopper   medium bowl   colander or strainer

PREPARATION

Combine   carrot, onions, red pepper, green pepper, and cabbage
           in bowl with salt and toss well.
Set   aside 2 to 3 hours.
Strain   liquid from vegetables and squeeze out excess mois-
           ture.
Add   celery seed, mustard seed, Tabasco, vinegar, and sugar.
Blend   very well.
Refrigerate   at least 3 hours before serving.

<small>VENEZUELA</small>   # HOLLOW CORN BREAD

<small>SERVINGS:</small> 12
<small>TIME NEEDED:</small> 55 minutes, plus baking time

INGREDIENTS

3 *cups water*	*margarine (optional)*
1 *tsp salt*	*grated white cheese (optional)*
2½ *cups white cornmeal*	

EQUIPMENT

2-qt saucepan   wooden spoon or beater   large heavy skillet
2 3-qt casseroles

PREPARATION

Boil water with salt in saucepan over moderate heat; then add
    cornmeal.

Beat mixture, which will be very stiff, until blended, remove
    from heat and cool.

Scoop about ¼ cup dough and shape into round about 3 inches
    across and ½ inch thick; repeat procedure until 12 individ-
    ual loaves have been formed.

Preheat oven to 400°F.

Heat ungreased skillet over moderate heat.

Fry rounds on both sides until crust forms on outside, about 5
    minutes each side.

Arrange fried bread rounds upright, standing on ends, leaning
    against sides of casseroles.

Bake about 1 hour, or until bread sounds hollow when tapped.

Traditionally these cornmeal rounds are served piping hot, split open,
and spread with butter and grated white cheese.

CHAD ## SWEET POTATO SALAD

SERVINGS: 8–10
TIME NEEDED: 15 minutes, plus boiling and chilling time

INGREDIENTS

4 large sweet potatoes
1 small onion, chopped finely
¼ cup peanut oil*
⅛ tsp salt

½ tsp black pepper
3 Tbs lemon juice
3 medium tomatoes

EQUIPMENT

large saucepan or soup kettle   chopper   large bowl

PREPARATION

Boil   unpeeled sweet potatoes in enough water in saucepan to cover them; cook until tender, but firm enough to slice.

Cut   cooled, peeled potatoes into slices about ¼ inch thick.

Combine   potatoes, onion, peanut oil, salt, and pepper in bowl.

Sprinkle   lemon juice on salad mixture.

Chill   at least 3 to 4 hours.

Slice   tomatoes just before serving; arrange as garnish around bowl.

*If peanut oil is not available or is undesirable, a light oil such as safflower oil may be substituted; a heavier oil, like olive oil, would be less appropriate.

COSTA RICA **PLANTAIN SALAD**

SERVINGS: 8–10

TIME NEEDED: 30 minutes, plus simmering and standing time

INGREDIENTS

3 qts water

3 large green plantains

¾ cup very finely chopped
    celery stalks

1 small green pepper, seeded
    and very finely chopped

1 medium onion, very finely
    chopped

¾ cup mayonnaise

⅛ tsp salt

¼ tsp black pepper

2 Tbs lemon juice

1 head leaf lettuce

EQUIPMENT

7-qt Dutch oven   slotted spoon   chopper   large bowl
paper towels

PREPARATION

Heat — water to boiling in Dutch oven over moderate heat; then add plantains.

Simmer — 15 to 20 minutes, uncovered, or until plantains are softened; then remove with slotted spoon and peel immediately.

Chop — plantains into very small pieces; combine with celery, green pepper, onion, mayonnaise, salt, black pepper, and lemon juice in bowl.

Mix — well and set aside for 30 minutes to allow seasonings and flavors to blend.

Wash — lettuce and let dry on paper towels.

Serve — mixed salad in large bowl lined with lettuce leaves, or as individual servings on bed of lettuce.

For a moister salad, add additional mayonnaise (or substitute yogurt); but it is better to start with a small amount and gradually add dressing to achieve preferred consistency.

FIJI   # TROPICAL CABBAGE SALAD

SERVINGS: 6–8
TIME NEEDED: 25 minutes

INGREDIENTS

¼ cup wine vinegar
⅛ tsp salt
⅛ tsp paprika
⅛ tsp dry mustard
⅛ tsp white pepper
½ cup olive oil

3 cups very finely sliced
  Chinese cabbage
¼ cup chopped green pepper
½ cup grated carrots
¼ cup chopped plain almonds
flaked coconut (optional)*

EQUIPMENT

pint jar with very tight lid   chopper   grater   large bowl

PREPARATION

Combine   wine vinegar, salt, paprika, mustard, white pepper, and olive oil in jar.

Tighten   lid on jar and shake vigorously.

Combine   cabbage, green pepper, carrots, and nuts in bowl and toss well.

Shake   salad dressing vigorously and pour about half over salad and toss lightly.

If salad is too dry, add more dressing as desired. Remaining dressing will keep if refrigerated.

*Customarily a generous amount of flaked coconut (as much as 1 cup) is added along with cabbage. However, a small amount (1 tablespoon or so) may be added to achieve a taste closer to the traditional, unless your diet does not permit it.

ITALY
CAULIFLOWER SALAD
WITH PIMIENTOS

SERVINGS: 4

TIME NEEDED: 45 minutes, plus soaking time

INGREDIENTS

1 medium cauliflower, trimmed
  of leaves
boiling water
pinch of salt
3 Tbs olive oil
1 medium garlic clove, minced
¼ tsp prepared mixed hot
  mustard

2 Tbs tarragon vinegar or wine
  vinegar
salt + ⅛ tsp salt
¼ tsp freshly ground black
  pepper
2 small, canned pimientos,
  diced
1 heaping tsp minced parsley

EQUIPMENT

medium saucepan   small skillet   pepper mill   serving bowl

PREPARATION

Soak   cauliflower in cold water for 15 minutes.

Divide   drained cauliflower into quarters; be careful not to break florets into small pieces; then pour boiling water over vegetable, barely covering the four segments; add pinch of salt.

Cook   just until tender; do *not* overcook or florets will fall apart.

Drain   cauliflower quarters and place close together in bowl to form whole head.

Heat   oil in skillet over low heat; cook garlic until soft but do *not* let it brown.

Stir   mustard, vinegar, ⅛ tsp salt, pepper, pimientos, and parsley into sauce in skillet; mix well until thoroughly hot.

Pour   hot dressing over cauliflower.

ITALY   # SPINACH AND ENDIVE SALAD

SERVINGS: 6–8
TIME NEEDED: 10 minutes

INGREDIENTS

1 lb fresh spinach, washed well   light salad dressing*
½ lb endive, washed well

EQUIPMENT

large bowl   paper towels

PREPARATION

Tear   spinach leaves into 2-inch pieces; drain on paper towels.
Break   endive leaves in half and let drain on paper towels.
Combine spinach and endive in bowl.
Pour   dressing over greens a very little at a time, just enough to
        moisten salad; too much dressing will make salad soggy.
Toss   salad in bowl lightly to coat leaves evenly with dressing.
Chill   briefly, about 5 to 10 minutes, before serving.

*The dressing typically used with this salad is a tarragon-vinegar dressing
(page 55).

MAURITIUS   **CARROT AND CUCUMBER
                      SALAD**

SERVINGS: 6
TIME NEEDED: 25 minutes, plus cooling time

INGREDIENTS

3 cups grated carrots   1 large onion, very thinly sliced
1½ cups grated peeled   6 Tbs olive oil
  cucumbers   4 Tbs white vinegar
6 hot chilis, seeded and minced

EQUIPMENT

whisk   large bowl   small bowl   grater

PREPARATION

Toss   carrots, cucumbers, and chilis lightly in large bowl; add
       onion and toss lightly again.
Stir   olive oil and vinegar vigorously in small bowl.
Whip   dressing with whisk until thick; then pour over salad
       greens and toss lightly.
Let stand   20 to 30 minutes in cool place.
Toss   again before serving.

This salad usually keeps well in the refrigerator for a couple of days.

RUSSIA   ## SALAD WITH YOGURT

SERVINGS: 6
TIME NEEDED: 20 minutes, plus chilling time

INGREDIENTS

2 cups torn salad greens
  (bite-size pieces)
1 large carrot, peeled and cut
  into long, thin strips
1 cucumber, peeled and cut
  into long, thin strips

1 large apple, peeled and cut
  into thin strips
2 tsps lemon juice
¼ tsp salt
¼ cup yogurt
3 tomatoes, peeled

EQUIPMENT

large bowl   processor or very sharp knife

PREPARATION

Combine   salad greens plus carrot, cucumber, and apple in bowl.
    Add   lemon juice and salt.
    Toss   salad ingredients and mix thoroughly; then add yogurt
           and toss lightly.
    Cut   tomatoes into quarters; arrange on top of salad.
   Chill   salad before serving.

TUNISIA   # BARBECUED TOMATO-PEPPER SALAD

SERVINGS: 6–8
TIME NEEDED: 40 minutes, plus chilling time

INGREDIENTS

3 large green peppers
3 medium onions
6 medium tomatoes
½ head lettuce or salad greens
3½ Tbs olive oil
1½ Tbs vinegar

¼ tsp salt
¼ tsp freshly ground black
  pepper
2 medium garlic cloves, minced
2 Tbs capers (optional)

EQUIPMENT

broiler   grinder or processor   medium bowl   wire whisk
pepper mill   paper towels

PREPARATION

Preheat   broiler; set rack 3 inches from heat source.
Broil   green peppers, onions, and tomatoes, turning them occasionally until brown all over, about 15 minutes; then let cool.
Wash   head of lettuce or enough salad greens to line serving bowl; drain on paper towels.
Remove   skins from peppers and tomatoes; cut all vegetables into 1-inch cubes; then process with coarse blade of processor or grinder.
Blend   olive oil and vinegar in bowl; beat with whisk until thick; then blend in salt, black pepper, garlic, and processed vegetables, and drained capers if desired; stir well.
Chill   1 hour before serving on bed of greens.

This dish is often served with one or more garnishes, including hard-boiled egg slices, lemon wedges, olives, anchovies, tuna fish, or crabmeat. If anchovies, olives, or other salty garnish is used, the amount of salt in the dressing can be reduced or left out altogether.

UNITED STATES   **CHANTAL
MUSHROOM SALAD**

SERVINGS: 6
TIME NEEDED: 30 minutes

INGREDIENTS

4½ Tbs Dijon mustard
4½ Tbs wine vinegar
¼ tsp salt
½ tsp dried oregano
½ tsp dried tarragon
¼ tsp freshly ground black
 pepper

⅔ cup olive oil
1 lb fresh mushrooms, sliced
 not too thin
2 Tbs chopped parsley

EQUIPMENT

medium bowl   large bowl   pepper mill   electric beater   chopper

PREPARATION

Combine mustard, wine vinegar, salt, oregano, tarragon, and pepper in medium bowl.

Blend well; then add olive oil very gradually; beat with electric beater until thick and smooth.

Pour enough dressing over mushrooms in large bowl to coat well; toss gently to make sure dressing is spread evenly.

Garnish with sprinkling of parsley.

HUNGARY **HORSERADISH SAUCE**

SERVINGS: 4–6
TIME NEEDED: 5 minutes

INGREDIENTS

1½ cups plain yogurt   grated peel from 1 large lemon
4 Tbs prepared horseradish, or
  very finely grated fresh
  horseradish root, if
  available*

EQUIPMENT

grater   small bowl or serving dish

PREPARATION

Combine   yogurt with horseradish; then add lemon peel.
  Blend   ingredients thoroughly before pouring on fish, or before
           setting on table for individual serving.

*Since fresh horseradish root tends to be very sharp, it should be used
sparingly. Add only 2 Tbs of grated fresh root, then taste sauce. If not sharp
enough, more may be added.

NEW ZEALAND   ## MINT SAUCE

SERVINGS: 8–12
TIME NEEDED: 15 minutes, plus standing time

INGREDIENTS

½ cup chopped fresh mint, or   2 Tbs sugar
  ¼ cup dried mint   ¼ cup mild vinegar, preferably
¼ cup hot water   wine vinegar

EQUIPMENT

chopper   small saucepan

PREPARATION

  Combine   all ingredients in saucepan.
     Cook   5 to 10 minutes over low heat, stirring to dissolve sugar.
Let stand   30 minutes in warm place.
    Serve   warm over braised, grilled, or roast meats (especially lamb), or over braised, broiled, or baked fish.

THE PHILIPPINES **SWEET-AND-SOUR SAUCE**

SERVINGS: 4–6
TIME NEEDED: 15 minutes

INGREDIENTS

4 Tbs vegetable oil
2 garlic cloves, minced
4 large onions, sliced
1-inch piece of fresh ginger,
   peeled and slivered
½ cup cider vinegar
¼ cup sugar

1½ cups chicken broth,
   skimmed
2 Tbs cornstarch
2 Tbs water
4 ozs pimiento, sliced into
   ½-inch strips

EQUIPMENT

12-inch skillet   small dish

PREPARATION

Heat   oil in skillet; add garlic and cook until well softened.
Add   onions and ginger; cook until slightly browned; then add
        vinegar, sugar, and chicken broth.
Heat   to boiling.
Combine cornstarch and water in dish, blending until smooth; then
        add mixture to hot sauce, stirring constantly until it thick-
        ens and comes to a boil.
Add   pimiento slices to sauce.
Remove sauce from heat and serve hot.

This sauce is customarily poured over fish dishes.

SOUTH AFRICA   **APRICOT SAUCE**

SERVINGS: 8–10
TIME NEEDED: 10 minutes, plus boiling and simmering time

INGREDIENTS

4 large onions, sliced
½ dried hot red chili, or ½ tsp
  crushed red pepper
3 Tbs sugar
3 Tbs curry powder
½ tsp ground turmeric

2 Tbs apricot preserve
2 cups vinegar
1 cup dried apricots
1 Tb flour
3 Tbs water

EQUIPMENT

2-qt saucepan   small dish

PREPARATION

Combine all ingredients except flour and water in saucepan.
    Heat to boiling over moderate heat; then reduce to low heat.
 Simmer 5 minutes.
   Blend flour and water in small dish just prior to serving.
    Pour flour mixture into hot sauce and blend well.
    Cook 2 minutes, or until sauce thickens.

This sauce is traditionally served on roast or barbecued lamb, but it
is also appropriate for grilled or roast pork or poultry.

SPAIN   # VINAIGRETTE DRESSING

SERVINGS: 8–10
TIME NEEDED: 10 minutes

INGREDIENTS

¼ cup red wine vinegar   *⅛ tsp black pepper*
¼ tsp dry mustard   *1 Tb grated onion*
pinch of salt   *¾ cup olive oil*

EQUIPMENT
2-cup cruet or jar with tight lid   grater

PREPARATION

Combine   vinegar, mustard, salt, and pepper in jar.
Shake   thoroughly in tightly sealed jar.
Add   onion and olive oil; shake very well.
Pour   into cruet to serve immediately, or store in tight jar in refrigerator.

SWEDEN   ## ZESTY DRESSING

YIELD: About ¾ cup
TIME NEEDED: 8 minutes

INGREDIENTS

½ cup olive oil   ⅛ tsp pepper
4 tsps vinegar   4 sprigs fresh dill, chopped
1½ tsps prepared mustard   very fine
⅛ tsp salt

EQUIPMENT

chopper   bottle or small jar

PREPARATION

Combine   all ingredients in jar.
  Shake   very well until ingredients are thoroughly blended.

This sauce is appropriate for serving on marinated or poached fish, as
well as on shellfish dishes.

SYRIA   # YOGURT SAUCE

SERVINGS: **6**
TIME NEEDED: **10 minutes**

INGREDIENTS

2 cups plain yogurt   *⅛ tsp salt*
2 tsps cornstarch   *pinch of black pepper*

EQUIPMENT

small saucepan   warming plate or tray

PREPARATION

Combine yogurt and cornstarch in saucepan.
  Heat to nearly boiling over moderate heat; do *not* boil.
   Add salt and pepper.
   Mix well and keep warm but only on very, very low flame, or
         on warming plate or tray.
 Serve warm.

Serve on vegetable, poultry, fish, or meat dishes.

UNITED STATES   **MOCK TARTAR SAUCE**

SERVINGS: 8–12
TIME NEEDED: 15 minutes, plus chilling time

INGREDIENTS

2 egg whites
2 Tbs skim milk
¾ tsp dry mustard
2 Tbs olive oil
½ tsp lemon juice
dash of cayenne pepper

2 Tbs capers, minced
1 small onion, minced
½ sweet-sour gherkin, minced
1 tsp very finely chopped
  parsley

EQUIPMENT

whisk or beater   medium bowl   chopper   jar with tight lid

PREPARATION

Beat   egg whites and skim milk.
Add   mustard, beating well, plus olive oil, lemon juice, and pepper.
Beat   until very smooth.
Add   capers, onion, and gherkin to sauce, blending thoroughly; then add parsley.
Chill   jar of sauce in refrigerator at least several hours before serving.

UNITED STATES   **SWEET-AND-SOUR SAUCE**

SERVINGS: 6
TIME NEEDED: 15 minutes, plus simmering time

INGREDIENTS

1½ cups sugar
1 cup white vinegar
1 cup water
¼ tsp salt
¼ cup chopped, seeded green pepper

4 tsps cornstarch
2 Tbs water
½ tsp paprika
2 Tbs chopped fresh parsley

EQUIPMENT

chopper   1-qt saucepan   saucer

PREPARATION

Combine   sugar, vinegar, 1 cup water, salt, and green pepper in saucepan.

Heat   to boiling over high heat; then lower heat.

Simmer   5 minutes.

Blend   cornstarch and 2 Tbs water in saucer; stir into sugar-vinegar mixture.

Cook   until slightly thickened, stirring constantly; then add paprika and parsley.

Serve   hot.

Sauce can be poured over roast meats or poultry, or served on the side.

UNITED STATES   **TERRACE GREEN
SAUCE**

SERVINGS: 3
TIME NEEDED: 10 minutes

INGREDIENTS

½ bunch (about ¾ cup) fresh
    watercress
½ cup fresh parsley
6 Tbs cider vinegar
⅛ tsp garlic powder

⅛ tsp salt
pinch of freshly ground black
    pepper
1 Tb light cream

EQUIPMENT

blender   small bowl   pepper mill

PREPARATION

Combine   watercress, parsley, vinegar, and garlic powder in
            blender.
Blend   at medium speed until fully pureed.
Transfer   to bowl; add salt and pepper.
Stir   light cream into puree and blend well.

Serve on seafood cocktails, or on marinated seafood, such as scallops
or shrimp.

WHITE SAUCE

SERVINGS: 4–6
TIME NEEDED: 10 minutes

INGREDIENTS

3 Tbs dry skim milk   1 cup cool water
2 Tbs flour*   1 Tb margarine (optional)
pinch of salt   pinch of paprika (optional)
⅛ tsp black pepper

EQUIPMENT
small bowl   double boiler   beater

PREPARATION

Combine skim milk, flour, salt, and pepper in bowl.

Stir ¼ cup water into milk mixture until smooth.

Set double boiler over moderately high flame to bring water in lower compartment to a boil; then pour rest of water into top of double boiler and add diluted milk mixture, plus margarine if a richer sauce is desired.

Beat mixture just until blended; stir constantly for about 5 minutes, until sauce thickens (water in bottom part of double boiler should be boiling).

Sprinkle paprika on top of sauce when serving to add a bit of color, if desired.

* For a thinner sauce, use a little less flour. For a thicker sauce, add an extra tablespoon of flour.

ALBANIA ## LEMON-CHICKEN SOUP

SERVINGS: 6–8
TIME NEEDED: 20 minutes, plus simmering time

INGREDIENTS

2 qts chicken broth, skimmed	4 tsps uncooked long-grain rice
8 black peppercorns	1 egg
1 large bay leaf	3 Tbs lemon juice

EQUIPMENT

4-qt Dutch oven   small bowl   wire whisk

PREPARATION

Combine chicken broth, peppercorns, and bay leaf in Dutch oven.

Heat to boiling over moderate heat; then add rice.

Simmer 10 to 15 minutes, covered, over low heat until rice is tender.

Beat egg in small bowl with whisk until frothy; then add lemon juice and continue beating well.

Pour small amount of hot soup into egg mixture, beating constantly to keep mixture frothy.

Add egg mixture to soup, beating constantly until frothy layer forms on top of soup; do *not* let soup boil or egg may curdle.

Serve immediately, while very hot.

AUSTRIA   **TYROLESE SPLIT PEA SOUP**

SERVINGS: 6
TIME NEEDED: 45 minutes, plus simmering time

INGREDIENTS

½ cup split peas	1 large potato, peeled and
¼ tsp salt	diced
1 qt water	1 large onion, sliced
2 Tbs margarine	1 Tb chopped fresh parsley
¼ cup diced celery stalks	1 Tb flour

EQUIPMENT

large saucepan   sieve or mill   chopper   medium saucepan

PREPARATION

Cook   split pleas, salt, and water in large saucepan until soft.

Strain   peas and reserve liquid; put peas through sieve; then return pureed peas to liquid.

Melt   margarine in medium saucepan and add celery, potato, onion, and parsley.

Cook   until tender; then stir flour into mixture and add to split peas.

Simmer   15 minutes.

DENMARK   **FRUIT SOUP**

SERVINGS: 6–8
TIME NEEDED: 45 minutes, plus standing time

INGREDIENTS

11 ozs mixed dried fruit   ½ cup sugar
4 ozs dried apple slices   ½ cup lemon juice
½ cup golden raisins   1 3–4-inch cinnamon stick*
½ cup dark raisins   10 whole cloves*
7½ cups water   ½ cup grape jelly
¼ cup tapioca

EQUIPMENT

4-qt Dutch oven   chopper   small cheesecloth bag (optional)

PREPARATION

Combine   all fruits and water in Dutch oven (use only 6 cups water
           if soup is to be served cold).
Let stand 30 minutes.
Remove   fruit and cut or chop into small pieces; then return to
           Dutch oven and heat to boiling.
Add   remaining ingredients except jelly.
Simmer   30 minutes, covered, on low heat, or until fruits are ten-
           der.
Add   jelly, stirring until melted.
Remove   cinnamon and cloves; serve warm or cold.

Fruit Soup will keep in refrigerator for several days and can be served
warm or chilled. To serve warm, reheat over very low flame. If soup
has thickened too much, add a little water.

*Tie cinnamon and cloves in small cheesecloth bag before adding to fruit
mixture for easy removal.

EGYPT **SPINACH AND YOGURT SOUP**

SERVINGS: 6
TIME NEEDED: 15 minutes, plus simmering time

INGREDIENTS

2 Tbs olive oil
1 small onion, chopped
¼ cup chopped scallions
10 ozs frozen leaf spinach
½ cup uncooked long-grain rice
¼ tsp salt
⅛ tsp freshly ground black pepper
5 cups water
2½ cups yogurt
2 garlic cloves, minced

EQUIPMENT

chopper   3-qt saucepan   medium bowl   pepper mill

PREPARATION

Heat oil in saucepan over moderate heat; add onion and scallions and cook until vegetables turn golden.

Add frozen spinach, rice, salt, pepper, and water; then heat until boiling.

Simmer on low heat for 15 minutes, covered, or until rice is tender.

Combine yogurt and garlic in bowl; then add to warm soup, beating steadily to blend well. Do *not* boil soup or yogurt may curdle.

Serve hot.

If the soup needs to be rewarmed, do so very carefully on very low heat to keep it from boiling and curdling.

FRANCE   # LEEK SOUP

SERVINGS: 6

TIME NEEDED: 35 minutes, plus simmering time

INGREDIENTS

2 Tbs olive oil

*2 lbs leeks, cleaned and cut
    into 1-inch chunks*

*¼ lb fresh spinach, washed,
    with stems removed*

1 cup shredded lettuce

*1 cup frozen green peas,
    thawed*

2 Tbs lemon juice

⅛ tsp salt

¼ tsp black pepper

1 qt chicken broth, skimmed

*¼ cup chopped parsley, celery,
    or mint*

EQUIPMENT

6-qt Dutch oven   blender   large bowl or soup tureen

PREPARATION

Heat   oil in Dutch oven over moderate heat.

Sauté   leeks until tender; then add spinach, lettuce, peas, lemon juice, salt, and pepper.

Cook   mixture until lettuce wilts; then add chicken broth and heat to boiling; then reduce to low heat.

Simmer   20 to 25 minutes, covered, or until leeks are tender.

Puree   some of hot soup in blender. Do *not* fill blender more than about one-third of the way at one time, and make sure that soup is not too hot; otherwise container may explode.

Pour   blended soup into large bowl and repeat procedure until all soup has been pureed.

Reheat   soup in Dutch oven, if necessary.

Garnish   each serving with parsley, celery, or mint.

MALAWI   ## RED BEAN SOUP

SERVINGS: 6–8

TIME NEEDED: 40 minutes, plus soaking and simmering time

INGREDIENTS

4–6 cups boiling water   2 large onions, chopped
2 cups red beans, washed   1 Tb flour
1–2 lbs soup bones, trimmed of   2 tomatoes, diced
  fat   ⅛ tsp salt
2 Tbs vegetable oil

EQUIPMENT

medium soup pot   chopper   masher or processor
medium saucepan   strainer*

PREPARATION

Pour   boiling water over beans in soup pot.
Boil   2 minutes; then remove from heat and soak for 1 hour or
        longer.
Add   soup bones and simmer 1 hour or more over low heat, until
        beans are very tender.
Remove soup bones and set aside.
Mash   beans in soup, or remove and put through processor; then
        return mashed beans to broth.
Heat   oil in saucepan and sauté onions until tender; then add
        flour, stirring continuously until mixture turns light brown.
Add   tomatoes, browned onions, salt, and reserved cooked
        bones to bean soup.
Simmer 30 minutes, adding more water if soup thickens too much
        to simmer readily.
Remove bones and spoon off fat that rises to top.
Serve   very hot.*

*Soup may be served as cooked, with bits of ingredients floating in it, or it can
be strained and served as a smooth, thick broth.

UNITED STATES   ## QUORUM
GAZPACHO

SERVINGS: 6
TIME NEEDED: 30 minutes, plus chilling time

INGREDIENTS

1 garlic clove, cut in half   *1 Tb white vinegar*
3 cups tomato juice, chilled   *2 Tbs lemon juice*
3 medium tomatoes, peeled,   *1 tsp Worcestershire sauce*
  seeded, and chopped   *dash of Tabasco sauce*
1 medium cucumber, peeled,   *¼ tsp salt*
  seeded, and chopped   *¼ tsp freshly ground black*
1 medium green pepper,   *pepper*
  seeded and chopped   *plain croutons (optional)*
1 Tb chopped fresh parsley

EQUIPMENT

medium bowl   chopper   blender

PREPARATION

Rub   inside of bowl thoroughly with cut sides of garlic clove.
Pour   tomato juice into bowl; add tomatoes, cucumber, green pep-
       per, parsley, vinegar, lemon juice, Worcestershire sauce,
       Tabasco, salt, and black pepper.
Blend   all ingredients well.
Return   soup to bowl or refrigerator container and chill.
Serve   well chilled.

Each portion may be garnished with croutons, if desired.

Vegetables

ORANGE CARROTS

SERVINGS: 4–6
TIME NEEDED: 15 minutes, plus boiling time

INGREDIENTS

6 large carrots, scraped and cut
   crosswise into 1-inch pieces
⅛ tsp salt
1½ tsps sugar

1 tsp cornstarch
¼ tsp ground ginger
⅔ cup orange juice
2 Tbs margarine

EQUIPMENT

scraper   medium saucepan   small saucepan   colander or strainer

PREPARATION

Boil   carrots with salt for 20 minutes, or until just tender.

Combine   sugar in small saucepan with cornstarch, ginger, and orange juice.

Cook   over moderate flame, stirring constantly, until sauce thickens and bubbles.

Boil   1 minute; add margarine, mix well; then drain carrots and toss lightly in sauce.

Serve   hot with sauce poured over tossed carrots.

CANADA   ## ONION CASSEROLE
WITH APPLES

SERVINGS: 6
TIME NEEDED: 30 minutes, plus baking time

INGREDIENTS

6 Tbs margarine	dash of black pepper
1 cup dry bread crumbs	4 medium tart apples, peeled,
3 Tbs maple syrup	cored, and sliced
4 medium onions, sliced	1 Tb cider vinegar
dash of salt	1 Tb water

EQUIPMENT

10-inch skillet   medium bowl   1½-qt casserole, lightly greased or
nonstick   small bowl

PREPARATION

Preheat	oven to 350°F.
Melt	3 Tbs margarine in skillet over moderate heat; then add bread crumbs.
Cook	until crisp; then remove to bowl and add maple syrup, mixing well.
Melt	3 Tbs margarine in skillet; add onions and cook until light brown.
Remove	from heat and separate into two equal portions.
Spread	half of onion slices in casserole and sprinkle with salt, pepper, and one-fourth of bread crumb mixture.
Layer	half the apple slices over crumbs.
Repeat	layers of onions, bread crumb mixture, and apples; then top with remaining bread crumbs.
Combine	cider vinegar and water in small bowl and pour over casserole.
Bake	1 hour, or until apples are tender and topping is lightly browned.

FIJI

SPICY EGGPLANT

SERVINGS: 8 (3 slices per person)
TIME NEEDED: 20 minutes, plus frying time

INGREDIENTS

1 large eggplant, peeled
½ cup flour
1½ tsps curry powder
⅛ tsp salt
½ small onion, chopped
2 garlic cloves, minced

1 small dried red chili (about
1-inch long), seeded and
minced
⅓ cup water
vegetable oil for frying

EQUIPMENT

chopper   small bowl   large heavy saucepan or griddle
cooking thermometer   paper towels   platter

PREPARATION

Slice   eggplant into thin rounds about ⅛–¼-inch thick.
Combine   flour, curry powder, salt, onion, garlic, and chili in bowl.
Stir   water gradually into flour mixture, adding a little more each time if needed to form a batter for dipping that is not runny.
Heat   enough oil in saucepan to 375°F to allow quick frying of eggplant slices.
Dip   eggplant slices in batter, a few at a time, letting excess batter drip off before frying 1 to 2 minutes on each side, until batter turns golden and eggplant is tender.*
Drain   on paper towels on platter.
Serve   immediately, while hot, as entrée, appetizer, or hors d'oeuvres.

*If batter gets too thick from standing while slices are being fried, add a little water to thin it enough for dipping rest of eggplant.

HUNGARY   **BAKED ASPARAGUS**

SERVINGS: 4–6
TIME NEEDED: 10 minutes, plus baking time

INGREDIENTS

24 steam-cooked asparagus   2 Tbs margarine
   stalks, drained   ⅓ cup yogurt
1 cup bread crumbs

EQUIPMENT

colander   large baking dish   small saucepan

PREPARATION

Preheat   oven to 350°F.
Slice   tender section of asparagus stalks into 2-inch segments.
Arrange   asparagus pieces on bottom of baking dish*
Spread   bread crumbs over asparagus.
Melt   margarine and sprinkle over bread crumbs; then cover with yogurt.
Bake   until crumbs turn light brown.

*If baking dish is not large enough for asparagus to be placed in single layer, divide pieces and make a second layer on top of first, reserving half the bread crumbs, margarine, and yogurt to top second layer. Baking time will increase slightly for double layer.

HUNGARY   ## PAPRIKA POTATOES

SERVINGS: 4
TIME NEEDED: 20 minutes, plus simmering time

INGREDIENTS

1 Tb margarine   ⅛ tsp salt
1 onion, finely chopped   ½ cup plain yogurt
¼ tsp paprika
4–6 medium potatoes, pared
  and diced

EQUIPMENT

chopper   medium saucepan

PREPARATION

Heat   margarine in saucepan; then add onion and paprika.
Cook   onion until soft and yellow; then add potatoes and salt.
Simmer covered, until nearly tender.
Add   few drops of water from time to time to keep potatoes from sticking to pan. Do *not* stir.
Add   yogurt when potatoes are done; stir very gently to spread yogurt, but do not break potato pieces.
Shake saucepan to keep potatoes from sticking while warming about 1 minute on very low flame.
Serve hot.

HUNGARY   **SWEET-AND-SOUR
STRING BEANS**

SERVINGS: 4–6
TIME NEEDED: 20 minutes, plus boiling and simmering time

INGREDIENTS

1¼ lbs string beans, cut into 2-inch pieces	*2 Tbs flour*
boiling water	*¼ tsp paprika*
¼ tsp salt	*1 Tb sugar*
2 Tbs margarine	*3 Tbs vinegar*

EQUIPMENT

medium saucepan   medium skillet   strainer or colander

PREPARATION

Cover beans in saucepan with boiling water and cook until almost tender; then add salt and set aside.

Melt margarine in skillet over moderate heat.

Blend flour into margarine, stirring until lightly browned; then add paprika, mixing until evenly distributed.

Add 1 cup liquid in which beans were cooked and blend until flour mixture is completely smooth.

Heat to boiling, stirring continuously until sauce thickens slightly; then add sugar and vinegar.

Drain cooked beans (discarding remaining liquid) and return them to saucepan; pour sauce over beans.

Simmer 5 to 10 minutes, uncovered, or until beans are done to desired tenderness.

Serve hot.

MAURITIUS # LENTILS WITH GINGER

SERVINGS: 4–6

TIME NEEDED: 40 minutes, plus simmering time

INGREDIENTS

½ lb lentils
1 qt water
¼ tsp salt
2 Tbs vegetable oil
2 medium onions, chopped
2 medium tomatoes, chopped

1 tsp minced fresh ginger
6 medium garlic cloves, minced
½ tsp dried thyme
2 Tbs chopped parsley
2 hot chilis, seeded and minced

EQUIPMENT

2-qt saucepan   chopper   10-inch skillet

PREPARATION

Cover lentils in saucepan with water and add salt.

Heat to boiling over moderate heat; then reduce to low heat.

Simmer 30 minutes, covered, or until lentils are soft but *not* mushy; then set aside.

Heat oil in skillet over moderate heat and cook onions until tender but not browned; then add tomatoes, ginger, and garlic, stirring occasionally until mixture thickens.

Add thyme, parsley, chilis, and cooked lentils with liquid, blending thoroughly.

Heat to boiling over moderate heat; then reduce heat and simmer 5 minutes, covered.

Serve hot.

MOROCCO   **SPICED CARROTS**

SERVINGS: 6
TIME NEEDED: 15 minutes, plus boiling time

INGREDIENTS

1 lb large carrots, scraped   dash of hot red pepper
pinch of sugar   ¼ tsp ground cumin
4 garlic cloves   6 sprigs fresh parsley
¼ cup wine vinegar   sprinkling of coriander seeds
⅛ tsp salt

EQUIPMENT

scraper   medium saucepan   small bowl   colander or strainer

PREPARATION

Cut	carrots lengthwise into 6 strips each; cover with water in saucepan and bring to a boil; then add sugar and garlic.
Boil	10 minutes, or until carrots are just tender.
Combine	vinegar, salt, red pepper, and cumin in bowl.
Drain	carrots; then pour marinade over them.
Serve	hot, garnished with parsley and coriander seeds.

SOUTH AFRICA

BRAISED STRING BEANS

SERVINGS: 6–8

TIME NEEDED: 15 minutes, plus braising time

INGREDIENTS

1 Tb vegetable oil

2 medium onions, coarsely chopped

1 garlic clove, mashed

1 chili pepper, very finely chopped

2 thin slices fresh ginger

dash of curry powder (optional)

20 ozs frozen string beans, thawed

EQUIPMENT

chopper   medium skillet or wok

PREPARATION

Heat   oil in skillet or wok (use less oil in wok) and brown onions over moderate heat.

Add   garlic, chili pepper, ginger, and curry powder if desired.

Mix   well; then add green beans.

Braise   slowly, just until beans are tender and begin to brown.*

*If mixture becomes too dry during braising, add more oil a very little at a time.

UNITED STATES   **CARROTS WITH NUTMEG**

SERVINGS: 3
TIME NEEDED: 30 minutes, plus simmering time

INGREDIENTS

8 medium carrots, scraped and cut lengthwise into quarters
1 cup water
pinch of salt
2 Tbs margarine
1 Tb sugar

½ tsp ground nutmeg
⅛ tsp salt
¼ tsp freshly ground white peppercorns
2 Tbs Grand Marnier (optional)

EQUIPMENT

scraper   1-qt saucepan   strainer   mill or blender   1-qt bowl
pepper mill

PREPARATION

Combine   carrots, water, and pinch of salt in saucepan.
Simmer   20 minutes, covered, over low heat, or until carrots are soft enough to process.
Puree   drained carrots in mill; discard water in saucepan.
Blend   margarine in saucepan with processed carrots, sugar, nutmeg, ⅛ tsp salt, and white pepper.
Reheat   seasoned carrots over very low heat, stirring constantly until thoroughly warm.
Serve   hot.

Traditionally, Grand Marnier is stirred into hot carrots just before serving.

AUSTRALIA ## BAKED FISH

SERVINGS: 6
TIME NEEDED: 20 minutes, plus baking time

INGREDIENTS

¼ cup grated or shredded firm
   low-fat cheese
1½ lbs fish fillets (whiting,
   flounder, or other non-oily
   fish)
¼ tsp black pepper
4 Tbs chopped shallots or
   green onions

½ lb mushrooms, sliced or 4½
   ozs canned mushrooms,
   drained and sliced
½ cup white wine (optional)
1½ tsps lemon juice
1 Tb chopped parsley

EQUIPMENT

grater or shredder   shallow baking dish (large enough not to crowd fillets)   chopper

PREPARATION

Preheat   oven to 450°F.
Sprinkle   cheese in shallow, oiled or nonstick baking dish.
Layer   fish fillets on top of cheese and sprinkle with pepper.
Layer   shallots and mushrooms on top of seasoned fish.
Pour   white wine over fish, if desired.
Bake   15 minutes.
Sprinkle   lemon juice on baked fish and let stand 2 to 3 minutes.
Sprinkle   parsley on top of hot fish just before serving.

CAMBODIA   **STEAMED FISH**

SERVINGS: 6
TIME NEEDED: 30 minutes, plus soaking and simmering time

INGREDIENTS

2 ozs rice noodles or rice
  sticks*
½ cup dried lily flowers*
3–4 cups water
2 garlic cloves, minced
1 Tb bean sauce*
2 Tbs peeled thinly slivered
  fresh ginger

1 tsp sugar
1 Tb fish sauce*
2 Tbs ground lean pork
1 whole red snapper, striped
  bass, or haddock, about 3–4
  lbs
6 sprigs parsley

EQUIPMENT

large bowl   mincer or chopper   collander or strainer
Dutch oven with rack or steamer large enough for whole fish

PREPARATION

Cover noodles and lily flowers in bowl with water; soak 30 minutes, or until ingredients are soft; then drain well.

Cut noodles into 3-inch lengths and cut each lily flower into 3 pieces; then return all pieces to bowl and add all remaining ingredients except fish and parsley; blend thoroughly.

Pour enough water into Dutch oven to fill it ½ inch deep; lay fish on rack, spreading noodle mixture evenly on top to cover fish completely.

Heat water to boiling over moderate heat; then reduce to low heat.

Simmer 20 minutes, or until fish flakes easily with fork.

Garnish with parsley.

*These items are usually found in oriental food stores and in some specialty food shops, or in specialty departments of supermarkets.

EQUATORIAL GUINEA STEAMED FISH

SERVINGS: 6
TIME NEEDED: 30 minutes, plus simmering time

INGREDIENTS

6 small sea bass or salt water
   fish such as flounder or
   porgy
6 medium onions, sliced
   ¼-inch thick

¼ tsp salt
¾ tsp black pepper
3 lemons, halved
12 sprigs parsley

EQUIPMENT

aluminum foil   7-qt Dutch oven

PREPARATION

Cut each fish into thirds.

Tear six 6-inch lengths of aluminum foil and place slices from half of each onion on center of each strip of foil.

Mix salt and pepper and sprinkle on onions; then lay 3 pieces of fish on each portion of onions; top with remaining onion slices evenly divided.

Squeeze one half lemon over each onion-fish layer and divide parsley sprigs evenly on top.

Bring opposite ends of foil together for each portion to make a fold, repeating with other ends of foil to make a "sealed" packet.

Pour water into Dutch oven and distribute packets of fish in pan without overlapping.

Heat to boiling at moderate heat; then reduce to low heat.

Simmer 1 hour, covered.

HUNGARY   **PAPRIKA FISH**

SERVINGS: 6–8

TIME NEEDED: 20 minutes, plus simmering time

INGREDIENTS

1 Tb margarine

2 large onions, chopped

1 tsp sweet Hungarian paprika

1 cup water

1/8 tsp salt

1/4 tsp black pepper

2 lbs fish (halibut, haddock, or other large fleshy fish), cut into serving portions

EQUIPMENT

chopper   large saucepan   strainer

PREPARATION

Melt   margarine in saucepan and add onions, frying gently until they become transparent; do not let them brown.

Add   paprika and water, stirring thoroughly; then add salt, pepper, and fish portions.

Heat   slowly to boiling; then lower heat immediately.

Simmer   about 45 minutes, shaking pan occasionally to keep fish from sticking; do not stir; add a little more water if sauce cooks down too much.

Transfer   fish portions carefully to platter and strain sauce over fish.

This dish is traditionally served hot with either boiled or mashed potatoes arranged on platter around fish.

MALAYSIA   SHRIMP WITH GREEN PEPPER

SERVINGS: 6
TIME NEEDED: 25 minutes

INGREDIENTS

2 Tbs vegetable oil
1 medium onion, very finely
  diced
3 scallions, very finely chopped
1 large green pepper, seeded
  and cut into thin strips
3 medium tomatoes, peeled
  and cubed
½ cup silvered, blanched
  almonds

¾ lb fresh shrimp, cleaned and
  deveined
½ tsp basil
½ tsp thyme
⅛ tsp salt
¼ tsp white pepper
2 Tbs flour
¾ cup yogurt or half-and-half
cooked rice (optional)

EQUIPMENT

chopper   medium saucepan or wok   small bowl

PREPARATION

Heat oil in saucepan or wok (use less oil in wok) and sauté onion
for 3 minutes; then add scallions, green pepper, tomatoes,
almonds, shrimp, basil, thyme, salt, and white pepper.

Simmer 3 minutes.

Mix flour and ¼ cup yogurt into paste; then thin with remaining yogurt.

Add yogurt sauce to shrimp mixture and cook just until boiling,
stirring constantly.

Serve immediately, while hot, preferably over rice.

MEXICO   **RED SNAPPER VERACRUZANA**

SERVINGS: 6
TIME NEEDED: 30 minutes, plus simmering time

INGREDIENTS

2 lbs red snapper fillets, or
   haddock, cut into serving
   portions
light sprinkling of salt
½ tsp black pepper
juice of 1 fresh lemon
3 Tbs vegetable oil

2 garlic cloves
3 medium onions, thinly sliced
1 1-lb can tomatoes
2 Tbs chopped ripe olives
2 Tbs capers
6 jalapeño chilis

EQUIPMENT

large skillet   juicer

PREPARATION

Rinse fish portions with cold water; then drain and season with
salt, pepper, and lemon juice.

Heat oil in skillet and add garlic, cooking until soft and flavor has
permeated oil; then discard garlic.

Cook onions in hot oil until yellow; then add seasoned fish,
tomatoes, olives, capers, and chilis.

Simmer a few minutes over low heat until sauce thickens and fish
is tender.

MYANMAR (BURMA)   **SHRIMP CURRY**

SERVINGS: 4

TIME NEEDED: 15 minutes, plus marinating time

INGREDIENTS

12 medium shrimp, shelled and deveined

1 Tb shrimp sauce or fish soy sauce

½ tsp turmeric

1 tsp paprika

3 cups minced onions

3 garlic cloves, minced

4 Tbs vegetable oil

1 cup tomato puree

1 cup water

EQUIPMENT

medium skillet or wok*   mincer or chopper

PREPARATION

Combine   shrimp, shrimp sauce, turmeric, and paprika.

Marinate   mixture for 1 hour.

Cook   onions and garlic in oil for about 2 minutes; then add shrimp mixture.

Cook   about 3 minutes, stirring lightly to make sure shrimp cook evenly.

Mix   tomato puree with water and add to shrimp mixture.

Cook   over low heat until sauce and oil separate.

Serve   hot, over rice.

*Cooking times will be shorter with wok.

THE PHILIPPINES   **SAUTÉED BASS**

SERVINGS: 4
TIME NEEDED: 20 minutes, plus simmering time

INGREDIENTS

⅛ tsp salt	¼ cup cornstarch
¼ tsp black pepper	¼ cup vegetable oil
1 2-lb sea bass, cut into serving	
portions	

EQUIPMENT

large plate or cutting board   12-inch skillet   paper towels
platter or warming tray

PREPARATION

Heat   oven to warming temperature, about 200°F.

Sprinkle   salt and pepper on fish.

Spread   cornstarch on plate or board and roll fish portions in corn-starch, covering evenly.

Heat   oil in skillet (use less oil in nonstick pan) over moderate heat until oil begins to form a haze; then add fish pieces, turning them over when golden, until both sides are done and fish flakes easily.

Drain   fish on paper towels and transfer to oven to warm until ready for serving with sauce.*

*This dish is traditionally served with a sweet and sour sauce (see page 137).

UPPER VOLTA

FISH STEW WITH VEGETABLES

SERVINGS: 6

TIME NEEDED: 45 minutes, plus simmering time

INGREDIENTS

3 Tbs vegetable oil

2 8-oz cans tomato sauce

1 medium onion, thinly sliced

¼ tsp red pepper

⅛ tsp salt

1½ lbs firm fish, cut into 6 portions

3 carrots, scraped and sliced ¼-inch thick

1 small head cabbage, thinly sliced

10 ozs frozen okra pods, cut in halves or sliced

10 ozs frozen green beans

1 cup uncooked rice

EQUIPMENT

12-inch skillet

PREPARATION

Combine oil in skillet with tomato sauce, onion, red pepper, and salt.

Heat to boiling; then add fish, carrots, cabbage, okra, and green beans; continue cooking, covered, until mixture boils again.

Simmer 5 minutes over low heat, then add rice.

Cook 25 minutes, or until rice is done; if mixture becomes too dry, add water but only a little at a time.

BAHAMAS BRAISED CHICKEN AND PORK

SERVINGS: 6–8
TIME NEEDED: 20 minutes, plus marinating and simmering time

INGREDIENTS

3-lb chicken, cut into serving
   portions
½ lb lean boneless pork,
   trimmed and thinly sliced
12 peppercorns

5 garlic cloves, minced
½ cup white vinegar
¼ tsp salt
1 bay leaf
1 qt water

EQUIPMENT

7-qt Dutch oven

PREPARATION

Combine   all ingredients in Dutch oven.

Marinate   1 hour at room temperature, turning meat occasionally so all portions are covered by liquid.

Heat   mixture over moderate heat until liquid boils; then reduce heat to low.

Simmer   1½ hours, covered, or until meat is very tender.

To make sauce from liquid, remove meat and thicken liquid by boiling it down to about half its volume. To keep fat content to a minimum, store sauce in refrigerator long enough for fat to rise; then remove.

COSTA RICA ## CHICKEN STEW

SERVINGS: 6
TIME NEEDED: 15 minutes, plus simmering time

INGREDIENTS

2 Tbs vegetable oil	1/8 tsp salt
4 lbs chicken portions	1 tsp paprika
1/2 chicken liver, chopped	1/2 cup water
1 large onion, chopped	1 cup dry red wine
2 Tbs flour	

EQUIPMENT

4-qt Dutch oven   platter   chopper

PREPARATION

Heat oil in Dutch oven over moderate heat and brown chicken portions evenly on both sides; then remove and set aside.

Cook liver and onion in oil until onion becomes tender; then sprinkle flour over hot mixture, blending thoroughly and stirring for 1 minute to prevent lumps.

Add salt, paprika, water, and wine.

Heat to boiling, stir well, and cook until mixture thickens slightly; then add chicken and reduce to low heat.

Simmer about 45 minutes, covered, or until chicken is tender.

Traditionally, this dish is made with guinea fowl and ingredients are fried in bacon drippings, with bacon slices added to the stew. To avoid using even lean pork bacon, 4 medium-thick slices of bacon substitutes, such as "turkey bacon" or "vegetarian bacon," may be added for a more authentic touch.

IVORY COAST   # CHICKEN WITH PEANUT BUTTER SAUCE

SERVINGS: 6
TIME NEEDED: 30 minutes, plus simmering time

INGREDIENTS

3 Tbs vegetable oil	1 Tb tomato paste
3-lb chicken, cut into serving portions	1 tsp paprika
	1 bay leaf
½ cup chopped onions	2 cups water
3 scallions, sliced	½ cup peanut butter
1 large tomato, sliced	

EQUIPMENT

large skillet or Dutch oven with cover   chopper
medium mixing bowl

PREPARATION

Heat   oil in skillet and brown chicken portions evenly on all sides.

Add   onions, scallions, tomato, tomato paste, paprika, and bay leaf to skillet.

Stir   all ingredients to mix evenly and coat chicken pieces; cook, covered, over low heat until sauce begins to bubble, about 5 to 10 minutes; then add water.

Simmer   15 to 20 minutes, covered, until chicken is tender.

Cream   peanut butter in mixing bowl with ¼ cup liquid from skillet, stirring well until peanut butter turns light and creamy; add more liquid if mixture is too thick; then pour sauce over chicken.

Simmer   10 minutes, covered, until flavor of sauce blends with chicken; serve hot.

For a less rich dish with fewer calories and less fat, remove chicken with slotted spoon and drain off sauce.

MALTA

ROCK CORNISH HEN
WITH VEGETABLES

SERVINGS: 6

TIME NEEDED: 30 minutes, plus simmering time

INGREDIENTS

3 Tbs margarine

2 1½-lb Rock Cornish hens

2 ozs lean smoked ham, trimmed and cut into narrow 2-inch-long strips

¼ cup chopped shallots

2 carrots, pared and chopped

½ lb turnips, peeled and diced

2 Tbs flour

2 cups chicken broth, skimmed

pinch of salt (optional)

¼ tsp black pepper

½ cup dry sherry

2 Tbs chopped parsley

EQUIPMENT

7-qt Dutch oven or large baking pan with cover   parer   chopper

PREPARATION

Melt   margarine in Dutch oven and brown hens evenly on both sides; then remove birds and set aside.

Add   ham, shallots, carrots, and turnips to Dutch oven and stir until lightly browned; then add flour, stirring for 1 minute.

Add   chicken broth, stirring constantly until mixture comes to a boil and thickens; then reduce heat to prevent scorching.

Add   salt if desired, pepper, ¼ cup sherry, and browned hens.

Simmer   1 to 1¼ hours, covered, or until hens are tender; then add remaining sherry.

Garnish   with parsley.

MOROCCO   **CHICKEN WITH ALMONDS**

SERVINGS: 6–8

TIME NEEDED: 45 minutes, plus boiling and simmering time

INGREDIENTS

3 ozs whole blanched almonds

⅛ tsp salt

⅛ tsp black pepper

2 cups water

2 Tbs vegetable oil

3½–4 lbs stewing chicken, cut into serving portions, with giblets

2 garlic cloves, minced

¼ tsp saffron

¼ tsp ground ginger

2 cinnamon sticks

dash of pepper

1 cup chopped parsley

EQUIPMENT

small saucepan   large skillet or 4-qt Dutch oven   paper towels
chopper

PREPARATION

Combine   almonds, salt, pepper, and 1 cup water in saucepan; bring to a boil over moderate heat; then lower heat.

Simmer   45 minutes.

Heat   oil in skillet, add chicken pieces, turning them to brown evenly on all sides until done; then remove and drain on paper towels.

Chop   giblets and place in skillet with garlic, saffron, ginger, and cinnamon sticks.

Cook   5 minutes, stirring occasionally; then add chicken pieces and sprinkle with pepper.

Simmer   30 minutes, uncovered; then add parsley plus 1 cup water; cook until chicken is almost tender.

Drain   seasoned almonds, add to chicken and continue cooking until chicken is tender, about 10 minutes.

NIGER
CHICKEN AFRICAINE

SERVINGS: 6
TIME NEEDED: 20 minutes, plus simmering time

INGREDIENTS

3 Tbs vegetable oil

3-lb stewing chicken, cut into
  serving portions

6 medium onions, sliced

6 medium red peppers, seeded
  and diced

⅛ tsp salt

¼ tsp black pepper

½ cup white vinegar

EQUIPMENT

7-qt Dutch oven   platter or bowl

PREPARATION

Heat   oil in Dutch oven over moderate heat, add chicken, turning pieces to all sides for even browning; then remove chicken to platter.

Cook   onions and peppers in Dutch oven until slightly browned; then pour all but about 2 Tbs fat from pan.

Return   chicken to pan and add salt, pepper, and vinegar.

Heat   to boiling; then reduce to low heat.

Simmer   about 1 hour, covered, or until chicken is tender.

SAUDI ARABIA　　**HONEYED CHICKEN**

SERVINGS: 8
TIME NEEDED: 15 minutes, plus baking time

INGREDIENTS

½ cup honey
⅛ tsp salt
¼ tsp black pepper
¼ tsp ground ginger
6 lbs chicken, cut into serving
　portions

½ lb Bing or large white
　cherries, pitted and halved
½ cup pistachio nuts, chopped
diluted lemon juice (optional)

EQUIPMENT

small bowl　pastry brush　jelly-roll pan
or large shallow baking pan　aluminum foil　chopper

PREPARATION

Preheat　oven to 400°F.
Combine　honey, salt, pepper, and ginger in bowl.
　Brush　each chicken portion with honey mixture on both sides;
　　　　then spread in pan without overlapping.
　Bake　25 minutes, or until chicken is tender,* basting occasion-
　　　　ally with drippings.†
Sprinkle　chicken with cherries and nuts.
　Bake　5 minutes, uncovered.

*If chicken darkens too quickly during baking, make a "tent" of aluminum
foil to cover pan for remainder of baking time.
†If drippings are very fatty, use diluted lemon juice instead to moisten
chicken.

THE UKRAINE **BAKED CHICKEN**

SERVINGS: 10
TIME NEEDED: 30 minutes, plus baking time

INGREDIENTS

6 lbs chicken, cut into serving
  portions
¼ tsp salt
½ tsp black pepper
3 Tbs flour
1 egg

2 egg whites
1 Tb water
2½ cups fine dry bread crumbs
3 Tbs vegetable oil
1 cup plain yogurt

EQUIPMENT

wax paper or large board paper towels 7-qt Dutch oven or
large baking dish beater small bowl platter or pie plate or
board 12-inch skillet paper towels

PREPARATION

Preheat oven to 350°F.

Wipe chicken portions dry and set on wax paper or board; then sprinkle with salt and pepper, and dust with flour, covering both sides.

Beat egg, egg whites, and water in bowl, and coat chicken pieces with egg mixture.

Spread bread crumbs on platter and roll chicken pieces in crumbs until evenly coated.

Heat oil in skillet over moderate heat and brown a few chicken pieces at a time, turning them until evenly browned on both sides; then remove and drain on paper towels.

Arrange pieces in Dutch oven or baking dish without completely overlapping.

Bake 30 minutes, uncovered; then spread yogurt over chicken.

Bake 20 minutes, or until chicken is tender.

This dish is best when served immediately.

ARGENTINA **MARINATED RANCH STEAK**

SERVINGS: 6–8
TIME NEEDED: 20 minutes, plus marinating and grilling time

INGREDIENTS

juice of 2 large fresh limes
½ cup lemon juice
1 tsp crushed red pepper
2 bay leaves
⅛ tsp salt
⅓ cup olive oil
½ cup water
3 lbs lean boneless 1-inch-thick round beef steak

EQUIPMENT

juicer   small bowl   large baking dish or roasting pan

PREPARATION

Combine lime juice, lemon juice, red pepper, bay leaves, salt, olive oil, and water in bowl.

Arrange round steaks in baking dish without overlapping and pour seasoning mixture over steaks.

Marinate 3 to 4 hours at room temperature, or overnight in refrigerator, turning steaks once or twice to spread seasoning mixture evenly.*

Grill 4 to 5 minutes on each side over hot coals or until cooked as desired, or under preheated broiler to desired doneness.

*Marinating steak serves two purposes: adds flavor to meat, and helps tenderize cuts that might otherwise be "tough." If beef is of less tender variety, longer marinating time is preferable.

CAMEROON   # BEEF WITH SPINACH

SERVINGS: 6–8
TIME NEEDED: 30 minutes, plus simmering time

INGREDIENTS

2 Tbs vegetable oil

2½ lbs lean stew beef,
trimmed and cut into 2-inch
cubes

2 small onions, sliced

20 ozs frozen leaf spinach,
partially thawed

⅓ cup canned tomato sauce

1½ cups beef broth, skimmed

1 Tb smooth peanut butter

¼ tsp black pepper

EQUIPMENT

4-qt Dutch oven   platter or shallow pan

PREPARATION

Heat   oil in Dutch oven over moderate heat and brown as many beef cubes on all sides as fit in pan without crowding.

Remove   browned cubes to warmed platter and repeat procedure with remaining meat cubes.

Cook   onions in remaining hot oil until lightly brown; then reduce heat and add spinach, tomato sauce, beef broth, peanut butter, and pepper.

Cook   until mixture comes to a boil, stirring occasionally; then add meat and lower heat.

Simmer   1½ to 2 hours, covered, or until meat is tender.

Serve   hot, traditionally with plantain or yams.

CANADA   **OVEN BOILED BEEF**

SERVINGS: 6–8

TIME NEEDED: 15 minutes, plus baking time

INGREDIENTS

4-lb lean rolled beef roast,*
  trimmed
3 onions, thinly sliced
2 carrots, pared and cut into
  thirds
1 bay leaf

1 tsp dried savory
¼ tsp salt
½ tsp black pepper
1 Tb honey
3 qts water

EQUIPMENT

7-qt Dutch oven   parer

PREPARATION

Preheat oven to 300°F.
  Place meat in center of Dutch oven and arrange onions and
         carrots around it.
   Add   bay leaf, savory, salt, pepper, honey, and water.
  Bake   4 hours, covered, until meat is very tender.*
 Serve   hot or cold, well drained of drippings from cooking liquid.

*Generally a shoulder roast is used but selecting the leanest possible cut of
beef is the major consideration. Baking time varies, depending on tenderness
of roast selected.

GERMANY   # SPICY POT ROAST

SERVINGS: 6

TIME NEEDED: 20 minutes, plus simmering time

INGREDIENTS

2 Tbs vegetable oil

2 lbs lean boneless beef, rump
or similar cut

1 garlic clove

1 tsp sugar

1 large onion, chopped

1½ tsps vinegar

1 tsp cinnamon

1 tsp ginger

¼ cup canned tomato sauce

⅛ tsp salt

¼ tsp black pepper

1 bay leaf

½ cup water

½ cup beer (optional)

EQUIPMENT

large Dutch oven   chopper   medium bowl

PREPARATION

Heat oil in Dutch oven; then add meat and brown well on all sides; then add garlic.

Combine sugar, onion, vinegar, cinnamon, ginger, tomato sauce, salt, pepper, and bay leaf in bowl; then add seasoning mixture and water to Dutch oven.*

Blend well, basting liquid over meat evenly.

Simmer 1½ hours, covered, over low heat until beef is very tender; turn meat over halfway through cooking so it does not stick or burn.

*Traditionally, beer is added to the pot roast at this stage.

GRENADA   ## MANGO PORK CHOPS

SERVINGS: 4
TIME NEEDED: 15 minutes, plus baking time

INGREDIENTS

¼ tsp black pepper
¼ tsp dried thyme
¼ tsp onion powder
½ tsp chopped fresh chives
4 thin pork chops, trimmed

2 tsps dark brown sugar
⅓ tsp ground cinnamon
1 underripe mango
rum (optional)

EQUIPMENT

small bowl   chopper   medium baking pan or baking sheet

PREPARATION

Preheat   oven to 350°F.

Combine   pepper, thyme, onion powder, and chives in bowl and mix
thoroughly.

Sprinkle   chops with seasonings on both sides.

Bake   45 minutes, or until nearly tender; make sure chops do
not overlap in baking pan.

Combine   brown sugar and cinnamon in bowl.

Slice   4 long strips from mango, each about ½ inch thick; set a
slice of mango on each chop.

Sprinkle   sugar-cinnamon mixture over mango strips.*

Bake   10 minutes more, or until sugar melts and mango turns
slightly brown.

For a variation, or if mangoes are not available, a thick slice of firm
peeled fresh peach may be substituted.

*Traditionally, a few drops of rum are also sprinkled on each chop.

HAITI
MARINATED VEAL CUTLETS

SERVINGS: 6

TIME NEEDED: 20 minutes, plus marinating and sautéing

INGREDIENTS

1 cup warm water
6 large, or 12 small, veal
  cutlets, pounded very thin
¼ tsp garlic powder
⅛ tsp dried thyme
2 Tbs chopped parsley

⅛ tsp black pepper
⅛ tsp salt
1 tsp sugar
½ cup orange juice
juice of 1 lemon
3 Tbs vegetable oil

EQUIPMENT

mallet   large bowl or roasting pan   small bowl   chopper   juicer
large heavy skillet

PREPARATION

Pour   water over meat in large bowl.

Mix   garlic powder and all remaining ingredients except oil very thoroughly in small bowl.

Pour   marinade over meat.

Marinate   4 hours, covered, in refrigerator; then drain.

Heat   oil in skillet until very hot.

Sauté   drained cutlets for only a few seconds on each side.*

*Very thin cutlets cook almost immediately on contact with hot oil and should be cooked quickly. If left in hot pan for more than 5 or 10 seconds on each side, veal tends to become tough.

IVORY COAST   **LAMB WITH OKRA**

SERVINGS: 6–8

TIME NEEDED: 60 minutes, plus simmering time

INGREDIENTS

3 Tbs peanut oil
3 lbs lean boneless lamb,
trimmed and cut into ½-inch
cubes
3 medium onions, very finely
chopped
1 lb fresh or frozen okra, sliced
1 cup beef broth, skimmed

2 Tbs chopped parsley
⅛ tsp salt
½ cup canned tomato sauce
4 Tbs chunky peanut butter
1 tsp chili powder
⅛ tsp cayenne pepper
6–8 servings cooked rice

EQUIPMENT

4-qt Dutch oven   chopper

PREPARATION

Heat   oil in Dutch oven and brown lamb cubes in batches, turning
them to brown evenly; then remove and set aside.

Cook   onions in Dutch oven over moderate heat, stirring occasionally until they turn golden brown; then add okra.

Cook   5 minutes; then add beef broth, parsley, and salt and heat
to boiling; then reduce to low heat.

Simmer   10 minutes; add tomato sauce, peanut butter, chili powder,
and cayenne pepper.

Simmer   5 minutes, stirring to blend well; add browned lamb cubes.

Heat   to boiling over moderate heat; then reduce to low heat.

Simmer   20 minutes, covered, or until meat is very tender.

Serve   hot over a mound of cooked rice.

SOUTH AFRICA ## BARBECUED LAMB

SERVINGS: 8–10
TIME NEEDED: 45 minutes, plus advance marinating, refrigerating, and broiling time

INGREDIENTS

2 garlic cloves
2 lbs lean boneless lamb, trimmed and cut into ½-inch cubes
4 bay leaves
⅛ tsp salt

½ tsp ground ginger
¼ tsp black pepper
2 Tbs ground coriander
½ cup skim milk
Apricot Sauce (optional)*

EQUIPMENT

large bowl   8–10 skewers

PREPARATION

Crush   garlic cloves inside bowl; then rub bowl with garlic and leave pieces in bottom of bowl.

Add   lamb, bay leaves, salt, ginger, pepper, coriander, and skim milk to bowl and blend thoroughly.

Marinate   overnight, covered, in refrigerator.

Pour   Apricot Sauce over meat and mix well.

Marinate   overnight again, covered.

Thread   skewers with meat, alternating with pieces of onion and apricot from sauce.

Broil   4 to 5 minutes on each side, 4 inches from broiler unit, or over coals, turning until meat reaches desired doneness.

*This dish traditionally calls for Apricot Sauce (page 138) to be used as part of marinating process, as well as for serving either over broiled skewered lamb, or as side dish for dipping.

SYRIA   **ROAST LEG OF LAMB**

SERVINGS: 6–8
TIME NEEDED: 15 minutes, plus roasting time

INGREDIENTS

2 large garlic cloves, minced	¼ tsp dried sage
¼ tsp salt	¼ tsp ground ginger
¼ tsp black pepper	¼ tsp dried thyme
¼ of large bay leaf, finely crushed	4-lb leg of lamb, trimmed
	1 Tb olive oil
¼ tsp dried marjoram	juice of 2 lemons

EQUIPMENT

small bowl   roasting pan   juicer   rack

PREPARATION

Preheat oven to 500°F.

Combine garlic, salt, pepper, bay leaf, marjoram, sage, ginger, and thyme in bowl.

Cut small gashes, 2 inches apart, over surface of meat.

Stuff blended seasonings into gashes in lamb; if any is left over, rub over outside; then brush olive oil over meat surface and set leg in roasting pan.

Roast 10 minutes.

Reduce oven to 350°F.

Roast meat about 2 hours, sprinkling occasionally with diluted lemon juice to keep moist; when done, remove to rack and let excess fat drip off.

Serve hot or cold, sliced very thin.

UGANDA   **CURRIED BEEF**

SERVINGS: 6–8
TIME NEEDED: 30 minutes, plus simmering time

INGREDIENTS

3 Tbs vegetable oil	3 large tomatoes, sliced
6 medium onions, sliced	2 tsps curry powder
2 lbs lean boneless beef, trimmed and cubed	⅛ tsp salt

EQUIPMENT

7-qt Dutch oven   small bowl

PREPARATION

Heat   oil in Dutch oven and cook onions until light brown; then remove to bowl.

Braise   meat in Dutch oven until each piece is browned all over; then add cooked onions and tomatoes, mixing well.

Simmer   45 minutes, covered.

Stir   curry powder and salt into mixture, and simmer 15 minutes, or until meat is tender.

This dish is frequently accompanied by mashed green bananas. Traditionally, it is also often served with a peanut sauce made from 3 heaping tablespoons of crisply roasted, finely ground nuts, or peanut butter, blended directly with the juices in the pan about 15 to 20 minutes before the meat is done. However, such a sauce may not be desirable to some because it increases the amount of fat.

UNITED STATES HAWAIIAN BEEF WITH SESAME SEEDS

SERVINGS: 2
TIME NEEDED: 20 to 30 minutes, plus marinating time

INGREDIENTS

¼ cup chopped scallions
2 Tbs chopped onions
1 Tb low-salt soy sauce
1 Tb sesame oil
1 Tb toasted sesame seeds
2 tsps sugar

¼ tsp minced garlic
½ lb lean trimmed boneless tender cut beef, trimmed and cut into strips 1 inch long by ¼ inch thick
1 Tb vegetable oil

EQUIPMENT

chopper   small bowl   10-inch skillet   platter

PREPARATION

Combine   all ingredients except beef and vegetable oil in bowl and mix well.

Marinate   beef in mixture for 20 minutes at room temperature, coating each strip well with sauce and stirring occasionally.

Heat   vegetable oil in skillet over moderate heat and add marinated strips in single layer, without overlapping.

Brown   lightly on one side, turning strips over to cook to desired tenderness; then remove to platter and repeat browning procedure until all strips are cooked.

Reheat   beef with marinade mixture until thoroughly warmed.

Serve   hot with sauce poured over beef strips.

UNITED STATES SEASONED LONDON BROIL

SERVINGS: 3–4

TIME NEEDED: 15 minutes, plus advance marinating and broiling time

INGREDIENTS

1 lb lean top round steak,
  trimmed

2¼ cups seasoned dressing
  (reduced calorie Italian,

French, or garlic-herb, or
Zesty Dressing on page 140)

EQUIPMENT

plastic refrigerating bag platter or shallow pan

PREPARATION

Place steak in plastic bag and add dressing.

Seal bag very tightly and shake thoroughly; then place on platter and refrigerate 12 to 24 hours before mealtime.

Remove from refrigerator shortly before mealtime and turn bag to distribute liquid evenly over meat before broiling.

Broil 7 minutes on each side; rack should be about 2 inches from heating unit.

Carve into thin slices, cutting diagonally across grain from top to bottom to avoid "stringy" portions.

BLUEBERRY CRISP

SERVINGS: 6
TIME NEEDED: 15 minutes, plus baking time

INGREDIENTS

⅓ cup granulated sugar
4 cups fresh blueberries,
  washed and destemmed
2 tsps lemon juice
2 Tbs margarine

⅓ cup brown sugar, firmly
  packed
⅓ cup flour
¾ cup quick-cooking oats

EQUIPMENT

1½-qt baking dish   medium bowl   mixing fork

PREPARATION

Preheat   oven to 375°F.
Sprinkle   white sugar on berries in baking dish and add lemon juice.
  Cream   margarine for topping and gradually add brown sugar, mixing well; then blend in flour, using fork for mixing.
   Add   oats and continue blending; then spread topping over berries.
  Bake   35 to 40 minutes.

For a more elaborate dessert, add a dab of nondairy or low-fat whipped topping (see page 199) to each serving.

GERMANY **SILVER SHELL TORTE**

SERVINGS: 6–8
TIME NEEDED: 15 minutes, plus baking time

INGREDIENTS

2 cups cake flour   ¼ cup sugar
⅛ tsp salt   ¾ cup margarine

EQUIPMENT

sifter   medium bowl   large springform pan   rack for cooling

PREPARATION

Preheat   oven to 400°F.
Sift   flour, salt, and sugar.
Cream   margarine into flour mixture, blending thoroughly.
Distribute mixture in springform to form a smooth, even ring.
Bake   10 to 15 minutes, or until ring has turned light brown.
Cool   2 minutes in springform; then remove and place on rack
           to cool completely.

The shell can be filled with fresh fruit, yogurt and fruit, Jell-O and
fruit, or any favorite filling.

IRELAND   **TEA BREAD**

YIELD: 2 8 × 5-inch loaves
TIME NEEDED: 35 minutes, plus standing and baking time

INGREDIENTS

1½ cups seedless raisins
1½ cups dried currants
1½ cups light brown sugar,
    firmly packed
2 cups strong hot tea
2⅔ cups flour

2 tsps baking powder
1½ tsps salt
1½ tsps ground cinnamon
½ tsp ground nutmeg
2 eggs

EQUIPMENT

2 large bowls   sifter   2 8 × 5-inch loaf pans, greased or nonstick
wire rack

PREPARATION

Combine raisins, currants, and brown sugar in bowl; then add tea.
    Set aside, uncovered, *at least* 4 hours (preferably 12 hours or
         overnight).
Preheat oven to 300°F.
    Sift flour, baking powder, salt, cinnamon, and nutmeg into
         second bowl.
    Add eggs to tea mixture and blend well; then add flour mix-
         ture, a little at a time, stirring only until batter is smooth;
         do *not* stir too much.
   Dust loaf pans with flour and divide batter between them.
   Bake 1¼ to 1½ hours, or until cake tester comes out dry when
         inserted into center of loaf.
   Cool 5 minutes on wire rack; then remove loaves from pans
         and cool to room temperature.

Tea Bread is traditionally sliced very thin and served with butter, but
jam or other spreads can be used.

JORDAN

SPICY RICE

SERVINGS: 6

TIME NEEDED: 15 minutes, plus boiling time

INGREDIENTS

1 cup farina
1 Tb ground cinnamon
1 Tb caraway seeds, pulverized
2 tsps aniseeds, pulverized
2 qts water

1½ cups sugar
½ cup cooked white rice
1 cup chopped walnuts,
*   almonds, or pine nuts*

EQUIPMENT

large saucepan   spice grinder or processor   chopper   custard cups

PREPARATION

Combine   farina, cinnamon, caraway seeds, and aniseeds in saucepan.

Add   water very slowly, stirring well; then heat to boiling, stirring constantly.

Cook   1 minute very rapidly, still stirring, and add sugar.

Boil   10 minutes, continuing to stir, and add rice.

Cook   until mixture reaches consistency of custard; then pour into individual custard cups.

Sprinkle   nuts on top as garnish.

Serve   hot.

POLAND   **PLUM FLUFF**

SERVINGS: 6
TIME NEEDED: 20 minutes, plus simmering and baking time

INGREDIENTS

1 cup red wine   4 egg whites
1 cup sugar   ½ tsp vanilla extract
2 lbs fresh plums, pitted

EQUIPMENT

medium saucepan   beater   medium bowl   2-qt baking dish or
6 individual casseroles

PREPARATION

Combine   wine and sugar in saucepan and heat to boiling, stirring
          constantly until sugar dissolves; then add plums.
Simmer   20 to 25 minutes, or until plums are soft.
Preheat   oven to 375°F.
Beat   egg whites until they stand in soft peaks, but do *not*
          overbeat.
Stir   sugar mixture gradually into egg whites, along with va-
          nilla.
Beat   until mixture is stiff and glossy; then pour hot plums with
          juice into baking dish.
Spread   meringue evenly over top of fruit.
Bake   about 12 minutes.
Serve   hot.

UNITED STATES   PECAN MERINGUE PIE

SERVINGS: 8

TIME NEEDED: 40 minutes, plus baking time

INGREDIENTS

4 egg whites at room
  temperature
½ cup granulated sugar
1½ cups unsalted soda cracker
  crumbs

1¼ cups very finely chopped
  pecans
2 cups sliced strawberries
2 Tbs confectioners' sugar

EQUIPMENT

medium bowl   beater   rolling pin or processor (for making crumbs)   9-inch pie plate, greased or nonstick   wire rack

PREPARATION

Preheat oven to 250°F.

Beat egg whites until frothy and soft peaks begin to hold their shape.

Add granulated sugar, 1 Tb at a time, beating until stiff peaks form.

Fold crumbs and 1 cup pecans very carefully into egg whites.

Spoon meringue mixture into pie plate, spreading it over bottom and sides carefully by using back of spoon.

Bake 45 minutes; then cool on wire rack until meringue is no longer warm.

Combine strawberries in bowl with confectioners' sugar, tossing lightly.

Spoon strawberry mixture evenly into meringue shell.

Decorate with nondairy whip to form a ring around inside edge of meringue.*

Sprinkle ¼ cup pecans over top.

*Traditionally, the ring is made with whipped heavy cream. If desired, whip chilled evaporated milk to use as topping.

UNITED STATES   **SNOW PUDDING**

SERVINGS: 4

TIME NEEDED: 25 minutes, plus chilling time

INGREDIENTS

1 cup orange juice	1½ Tbs plain gelatin
½ cup sugar	¼ cup cold water
3 Tbs lemon juice	4 egg whites
⅛ tsp salt	
½ tsp anisette, or 2–3 drops oil of angelica	

EQUIPMENT

medium saucepan   small bowl   beater   small casserole or mold, lightly oiled or nonstick

PREPARATION

Heat   orange juice in saucepan; do *not* let boil; then add sugar, stirring constantly, plus lemon juice, salt, and anisette.

Stir   gelatin into cold water and add to orange juice, stirring well until smooth; then cool mixture until it gets quite thick.

Beat   egg whites until stiff; then add cooled gelatin mixture very gradually, beating constantly.

Pour   pudding into casserole.

Chill   several hours in refrigerator, or overnight, until set.

Serve   chilled.

Snow Pudding is often served with a custard-sauce topping. If this is not feasible for dietary reasons, serve with nondairy or low-fat topping (page 199), or with slices of fresh fruit, such as strawberries.

UNITED STATES **WHIPPED TOPPING**

SERVINGS: 3–4
TIME NEEDED: 10 minutes, plus chilling time

INGREDIENTS

½ cup ice-cold water *1 Tb sugar*
1 Tb lemon juice *¼ tsp vanilla extract*
½ cup dry skim milk

EQUIPMENT

juicer   large mixing bowl   beater or wire whisk

PREPARATION

Combine water, lemon juice, and skim milk in bowl.
Beat until mixture thickens; then add sugar and vanilla and continue beating until well mixed and well thickened.
Chill before serving.

YUGOSLAVIA   **PLUM PIE FILLING**

SERVINGS: 12
TIME NEEDED: 30 minutes

INGREDIENTS

¾ cup sugar
3½ lbs ripe tart plums, pitted
  and sliced into rounds about
  ¼ inch thick
1 lb walnuts or pecans, quite
  finely ground

1 Tb cinnamon
rind of 1 lemon, grated
3 Tbs margarine

EQUIPMENT

medium bowl   grater   grinder or chopper   small bowl   small saucepan

PREPARATION

Sprinkle   sugar over plums* in small bowl.
    Mix   nuts, cinnamon, and lemon rind in large bowl and add sugared plums.
   Line   pastry shell with spiced plums.
   Melt   margarine.
Drizzle   margarine over plum filling and pie pastry and bake according to pastry directions.

Baking time depends on whether pie is made with a single crust or two crusts. Traditionally, Slovenian plum pie is made with a very rich pastry arranged in layers. The filling is divided between two layers, and there is a third, top layer of pastry. The pie is trimmed ½ inch beyond the edge of the pie plate, and edges are folded under, pressed until sealed, and then fluted with a fork. Usually a beaten egg is brushed over top of dough. If pie is made this way, bake about an hour in an oven preheated to 375°F.

*If plums are very sour, use 1 cup sugar; if plums are sweet, use ½ cup sugar.

PART III

Reduced Salt Recipes

INTRODUCTION

History tells us that in many parts of the world where salt was scarce or too costly, primitive people survived because they met the body's need for sodium by consuming fish, animals, or vegetables, all of which contain sodium.

This means an appreciable amount of sodium is already present in many foods prior to cooking. For example, a quarter-pound portion of raw broiling chicken contains 75 milligrams of sodium; a pound of whole raw shrimp has 438 milligrams, and a one-pound, raw porter-house steak has about 268 milligrams of sodium.

That's why it's important to realize the way you cook such foods can determine how much of the sodium is left to be consumed. It can prove to be a catch-22 situation. For instance, if the shrimp is marinated in a salty mixture, not only will the original sodium likely remain in the shellfish, but even more may be absorbed from the marinade. Similarly, if the poultry is roasted or broiled on a rack to let the fat and juices drain off, some sodium is likely to escape. But if the drippings are then used to make a gravy to pour over rice or potatoes, some additional sodium is bound to be ingested.

But the real shocker comes in checking the total amount of sodium in commercially prepared foods. The third edition of the *Barbara Kraus Complete Guide to Sodium* reveals that a well-known "extra helping" brand of frozen steak dinner has 2,175 milligrams of sodium. A whole teaspoon of common table salt has less, about 2,131 milligrams. As for desserts, popular brands of frozen apple or cherry pie—though they often taste deceptively sweet—may have as much as 500 or more milligrams of sodium in the 8-ounce size.

In looking at the overall picture, it would be a mistake to ignore the fact that sodium, like cholesterol, has both a good and bad side. On the plus side, it's essential in many bodily functions, including heart action, the transmission of nerve impulses, and the normal operation of several vital enzyme systems. It plays a key role in the regulation of the level of water retained in our tissues and bloodstream, as well as the amount we excrete.

On the negative side, medical evidence strongly suggests that too much sodium in our foods may be a contributing and/or complicating factor in the development of high blood pressure. Contrary to a widespread impression that high blood pressure (hypertension) occurs in later life, it can actually start at any age, even childhood, often very silently and insidiously. Since high blood pressure unquestionably increases the risk for coronary heart disease and for a stroke, more and more doctors and nutritionists now urge that we choose foods with less sodium.

As yet there is no specific recommended minimal amount of sodium that should be consumed daily to meet the physiological needs of healthy individuals. The National Research Council has suggested that under normal circumstances the estimated safe and adequate daily intake is in the range of about 1,100–3,300 milligrams. That level allows for some salt to be used in cooking but not at the table.

Accordingly, it's up to each individual to make the choice whether to ban salt from the kitchen or from the table—or both. But in any case, we caution readers not to undertake a salt-free or highly salt-restricted diet unless they do so under a physician's supervision. We also urge careful reading of labels on all processed foods. To help consumers keep track of exactly how much sodium they get from processed foods, the American Medical Association and other health-oriented organizations have encouraged food companies to provide precise information on their labels. Many have already done so with both frozen and canned products.

Yet that's only one side of the coin. Fresh foods, including meats, fish, poultry, fruits, and vegetables, as well as bakery goods, also contribute to our daily intake of sodium. And there is as yet no way of providing accurate nutrient labeling for these common items. This means that consumers who want to monitor sodium intake accurately will have to do it on their own by checking the sodium content of unlabeled items in a reference source such as the *Barbara Kraus Complete Guide to Sodium.*

For all these reasons, we've designed this section to acquaint you with some unusual and exciting recipes that don't require significant amounts of added salt. We hope they will pique your interest and help you to painlessly cross the threshold into a new experience—cooking with less salt than called for in most traditional dishes.

ALBANIA **MINT-FLAVORED MEATBALLS**

SERVINGS: 12–18 (about 3 dozen meatballs)
TIME NEEDED: 30 minutes, plus marinating and browning time

INGREDIENTS

3 Tbs chopped fresh mint
2 large garlic cloves, minced
1 lb lean ground lamb
2 eggs
1 cup fresh bread crumbs

2 tsps flour
1 tsp ground cinnamon
⅛ tsp salt
¼ tsp black pepper
⅓–½ cup vegetable oil

EQUIPMENT

chopper   medium bowl   beater or whisk   small bowl
10-inch skillet   paper towels

PREPARATION

Combine   mint, garlic, and lamb in medium bowl.
Beat   eggs in small bowl; then add to meat, along with all remaining ingredients except oil.
Marinate   overnight in refrigerator, covered.*
Shape   spoonfuls of meat mixture into 1-inch balls.
Heat   oil in skillet over moderate heat.
Brown   batches of meatballs about 4 to 6 minutes, turning to cook evenly.
Drain   on paper towels and serve hot as individual portions, or keep on warming tray for buffets.

*If time does not permit overnight refrigeration, keep meat mixture refrigerated at least a few hours, or if in a great hurry, keep at room temperature, covered, for 1 to 2 hours. But without overnight refrigeration, flavors will not blend as fully and meat will not be quite as tasty.

CZECHOSLOVAKIA   **HAM ROLLS**

SERVINGS: 12
TIME NEEDED: 15 minutes

INGREDIENTS

12 *thin slices cooked trimmed*
    ham, preferably fresh,
    unsalted
1 *jar horseradish sauce,*
    prepared, creamed variety

2 *medium apples, sliced into 6*
    wedges each
2 *Tbs lemon juice*

EQUIPMENT

toothpicks   small bowl

PREPARATION

Spread   each slice of ham with horseradish sauce.
  Dip   apple wedges into lemon juice in bowl.
 Roll   each slice of seasoned ham and fasten with toothpick; then
           fasten apple wedge onto top of each ham roll.

DENMARK　　**BEET AND APPLE RELISH**

SERVINGS: 2–3

TIME NEEDED: 15 minutes, plus chilling time

INGREDIENTS

½ cup peeled chopped apples　　*3 Tbs mayonnaise*
½ cup home cooked or canned　　*1 Tb honey*
　julienne beets　　*⅛ tsp salt*
¼ cup plain yogurt

EQUIPMENT

peeler　chopper　2 small bowls

PREPARATION

Combine　apples with beets.
　Blend　yogurt with remaining ingredients in second bowl.
　　Pour　yogurt dressing over apple-beet mixture; stir lightly but blend thoroughly.
　　Chill　3 hours or longer before serving.

EGYPT   **CHICK PEA LOGS**

SERVINGS: 8–12 (about 18 logs)
TIME NEEDED: 60 minutes

INGREDIENTS

2 cups cooked chick peas,   ⅛ tsp dried thyme
  drained   2 Tbs dried bread crumbs
⅛ tsp salt   1 egg
¼ tsp black pepper   1 Tb olive oil
¼ tsp cayenne pepper   2 Tbs flour
⅛ tsp dried basil   vegetable oil for frying

EQUIPMENT

mill or processor   large bowl   2-qt saucepan
cooking thermometer   paper towels

PREPARATION

Press chick peas through mill into large bowl and add salt, black
pepper, cayenne pepper, basil, thyme, bread crumbs, egg,
and olive oil, blending thoroughly.

Scoop 2 Tbs of mixture and shape into rounded log, about 2 inches
long and ¾ inch thick; repeat using rest of mixture.

Dust logs lightly with flour.

Heat vegetable oil in saucepan to about 375°F; use enough oil for
quick, deep-frying.

Brown 5–6 logs at a time, about 3 to 4 minutes, until golden in color;
repeat procedure until all logs are browned.

Drain cooked logs well on paper towels.

Serve hot, as appetizer.

Chick peas in this form, or as larger croquettes, are as popular in the
Middle East as hot dogs or hamburgers are in the United States. Such
falafel dishes are also served with bread as a sandwich, or even as a
main dish.

ESTONIA **ROLLS WITH PUFFED CHEESE**

SERVINGS: 8 or 16*
TIME NEEDED: 15 minutes, plus baking time

INGREDIENTS

1 cup creamed cottage cheese† 2 egg whites
3 Tbs softened margarine   4 long hard rolls (French,
pinch of salt   Vienna, Mexican bolillos, or
2 tsps caraway seeds   crusty rye)
1 Tb sugar
½ cup sour cream or low-salt
  yogurt

EQUIPMENT

medium bowl   beater or whisk   jelly-roll pan or cookie sheet

PREPARATION

Preheat oven to 425°F.

Combine cottage cheese, margarine, salt, caraway seeds, sugar, and sour cream in bowl.

Whip egg whites until peaks form; then fold into cheese mixture.

Split rolls into halves,* and spread about 3–4 Tbs cheese mixture evenly across each half, dividing mixture evenly among the 8 halves.

Bake 10 to 15 minutes in jelly-roll pan, or until cheese spread has puffed up and turned light brown on top; then slash each puffed roll at a slant across the middle.

Serve immediately, while piping hot.

*To serve as "finger food" on a buffet table, cut each roll in quarters to make sixteen smaller servings.
†Several types of "lite," reduced salt, or low-salt products are now available.

MALAWI   **CURRIED RICE BALLS**

SERVINGS: 12–15 (about 30 small balls)
TIME NEEDED: 45 minutes

INGREDIENTS

2 Tbs margarine   ⅛ tsp salt
1 medium onion, chopped   4 Tbs flour
2 cups cooked long-grain rice   1 egg
¾ tsp curry powder   peanut oil for frying

EQUIPMENT

chopper   10-inch skillet   medium bowl   2-qt saucepan
cooking thermometer   paper towels   ovenproof platter or
baking sheet

PREPARATION

  Melt margarine in skillet over low heat; add onion and cook
          until tender and light brown; then let cool.
Combine rice, curry powder, salt, flour, egg, and cooked onion in
          bowl; blend thoroughly.
 Scoop spoonfuls of mixture and shape into 1-inch balls.
Preheat oven to 200°F.
  Heat enough peanut oil in saucepan to allow quick deep-frying
          at 350°F.
   Fry 5–6 balls at a time, about 2 minutes, until golden color all
          over, repeating procedure with remaining balls; drain on
          paper towels.
Transfer drained rice balls to platter in oven to keep warm.*

*Customarily served warm, but may also be served cold.

SCOTLAND   ## OAT SCONES

SERVINGS: 12
TIME NEEDED: 25 minutes, plus baking time

INGREDIENTS

1½ cups all-purpose flour   *pinch of salt*
1½ cups uncooked oats   *⅔ cup unsalted margarine*
2–3 Tbs sugar   *⅓ cup milk*
1 Tb baking powder   *1 egg*
1 tsp cream of tartar   *½ cup currants or raisins*

EQUIPMENT

medium bowl   small saucepan   small bowl   whisk   pastry board
cookie sheet

PREPARATION

Preheat   oven to 425°F.
   Stir   flour, oats, sugar, baking powder, cream of tartar, and salt
          in medium bowl.
   Melt   margarine in saucepan over low heat; then remove from
          heat and add milk.
   Beat   egg lightly in small bowl; then add to milk mixture and
          combine with dry ingredients, mixing well; then add cur-
          rants and mix well again.
  Empty   batter onto lightly floured board; shape dough into large,
          round 9-inch cake; then cut circle of dough into 12 wedges.
 Grease   cookie sheet lightly and transfer wedges to sheet; do not
          overlap.
   Bake   12 minutes, or until light golden brown.
  Serve   hot.

These scones are usually served with honey, but a bitter marmalade,
jam, or similar spread are equally popular.

SPAIN   **SHRIMP SERAPICO**

SERVINGS: 6
TIME NEEDED: 30 minutes, plus baking time

INGREDIENTS

6 ozs low-salt soft cream
cheese or farmer's cheese
3 ozs Roquefort cheese or
Danish blue cheese
4 ozs pimientos, chopped

2 lemons
1 lb medium shrimp, peeled
and cleaned
6 Tbs dry white wine

EQUIPMENT

chopper   medium bowl   aluminum foil   baking sheet

PREPARATION

Preheat oven to 400°F.
Combine both cheeses with pimientos, blending thoroughly.
Cut 6 pieces aluminum foil, each 8 inches long.
Cut each lemon into 3 generous slices.
Spread center of each piece of foil with cheese mixture, dividing evenly; add one-sixth portion of shrimp to top of cheese portions; then top with lemon slices.
Fold opposite ends of foil together, making ½-inch fold and repeating procedure with other ends, but leaving small temporary opening for pouring 1 Tb wine into each packet before sealing.
Bake packets on baking sheet for 20 to 25 minutes, or until shrimp are done.
Serve immediately, while hot.

UNITED STATES   # NEW ENGLAND PUMPKIN BREAD

SERVINGS: 16

TIME NEEDED: 30 minutes, plus baking time

INGREDIENTS

vegetable oil for greasing
  bread pans
3 cups sifted white flour
2 tsps baking powder
2 tsps baking soda
2 tsps ground cinnamon

¼ tsp salt
1¾ cups sugar
1¼ cups vegetable oil
4 eggs
1 14–15-oz-can unseasoned
  pumpkin*

EQUIPMENT

large bowl   medium bowl   2 large or 3 small bread pans   beater

PREPARATION

Preheat   oven to 350°F.

Oil   bread pans lightly, or use nonstick pans.

Combine   flour, baking powder, baking soda, cinnamon, and salt in large bowl.

Combine   sugar and vegetable oil in medium bowl; gradually beat 1 egg at a time into sugar mixture; then add pumpkin.

Add   egg batter from medium bowl gradually to dry ingredients in large bowl, stirring or beating continuously to blend thoroughly.

Bake   1 hour (less if small bread pans are used) until cake tester comes out dry in middle of loaf.

*Use only plain canned or fresh homemade pumpkin. Do not use canned pumpkin-pie filling, which comes already seasoned.

UNITED STATES   **ZESTY CRANBERRY
RELISH**

SERVINGS: 12–16
TIME NEEDED: 15 minutes

INGREDIENTS

1 lb fresh cranberries, washed
  and destemmed
2 large oranges, quartered and
  seeded
grated rind of 1 lemon (use
  only outer rind, not white
  membrane)

1 cup honey
¾ cup sugar

EQUIPMENT

chopper or processor   grater   large bowl

PREPARATION

Chop cranberries and oranges, including rinds, coarsely.
Add remaining ingredients and mix thoroughly.
Chill before serving.

Salads

ISLAND LOBSTER SALAD

SERVINGS: 6

TIME NEEDED: 15 minutes, plus chilling time

INGREDIENTS

¾ lb cooked lobster meat, fresh, not canned, diced into ½-inch pieces

2 Tbs diced peeled cucumber

2 Tbs diced onion

2 Tbs diced celery stalks

2 Tbs diced green pepper

3 Tbs lemon juice

¼ cup mayonnaise or salad dressing*

pinch of salt

dash of Tabasco sauce

EQUIPMENT

medium bowl

PREPARATION

Combine all ingredients in bowl, blending well.

Chill at least 30 minutes before serving.

Serve on toast rounds, salt-free crackers, or similar breads, or as individual portions on bed of lettuce.

*Low-salt salad dressings are now available, or prepare a homemade dressing with low salt or no salt in advance.

BULGARIA   **MIXED VEGETABLE SALAD**

SERVINGS: 6
TIME NEEDED: 60 minutes, plus chilling time

INGREDIENTS

½ tsp salt
1 medium cucumber, thinly sliced
3 green peppers
4 medium tomatoes, peeled and sliced

1 medium onion, sliced
¼ cup wine vinegar or lemon juice
⅛ tsp salt
⅛ tsp black pepper
⅓ cup olive oil

EQUIPMENT

medium bowl   broiler   large bowl   whisk

PREPARATION

Sprinkle   ½ tsp salt on cucumber slices in medium bowl and let stand 20 minutes; then rinse salt from slices and drain liquid completely.

Preheat   broiler.

Prepare   green peppers by removing tops, seeds, and membranes and cutting peppers into quarters.

Broil   peppers about 4 inches from heat source until skin bubbles and begins to scorch; then cool and peel off skins; cut each quarter in half lengthwise.

Combine   cucumber slices in large bowl with peppers, tomatoes, and onion.

Mix   vinegar in small bowl with remaining salt and pepper; then beat well with whisk and add oil gradually, beating continuously until dressing thickens.

Pour   desired amount of dressing over salad.

Chill   1 to 2 hours before serving.

JAPAN   # CHICKEN SALAD WITH
GOLDEN DRESSING

SERVINGS: 6
TIME NEEDED: 45 minutes, plus cooling time

INGREDIENTS

¼ tsp salt	1 egg yolk
1 medium cucumber, thinly sliced	1 tsp cornstarch
½ cup water	1 tsp sugar
½ lb raw boneless chicken breasts	⅛ tsp salt
1 medium tomato, peeled and cut into 6 slices	4 tsps rice vinegar
	2 Tbs water

EQUIPMENT

10-inch skillet   small bowl   paper towels   salad plates   whisk or beater

PREPARATION

Sprinkle   ¼ tsp salt on cucumber slices in bowl and let stand 20 minutes; then rinse slices with water, drain, and dry on paper towels.

Boil   ½ cup water in skillet, lower heat, add chicken breasts, and simmer 20 minutes, covered, or until meat is done; then cool and cut into thin strips.

Arrange   salad plates with equal amounts of cucumber, chicken, and tomato slices.

Beat   egg yolk, cornstarch, sugar, salt, rice vinegar, and water in bowl until well blended.

Spoon   dressing over each serving.

SPAIN   **ANDALUSIAN TOMATO SALAD**

SERVINGS: 6
TIME NEEDED: 30 minutes, plus chilling time

INGREDIENTS

4 large tomatoes, sliced
7–8 ozs canned roasted
  peppers or pimientos, sliced
  into thin strips
⅓ cup vinaigrette salad
  dressing*

1 small cucumber, thinly sliced
1 medium apple, peeled and
  sliced
¼ cup chopped parsley
2 hard-boiled eggs, cut into
  wedges

EQUIPMENT

salad bowl   peeler   chopper

PREPARATION

Combine tomato and pepper slices in bowl, tossing lightly.

Sprinkle salad dressing over tomato-pepper mixture, tossing lightly.

Arrange cucumber slices around edge of bowl, scatter diced apple over salad mixture, and sprinkle parsley over entire salad.

Arrange egg wedges around outside of salad.

Serve cold immediately, or after chilling 15 to 30 minutes.†

*This salad is customarily served with a vinaigrette dressing (page 139).
† If salad is not served immediately, the diced apple should be tossed with a little lemon juice or a commercial fresh fruit preservative to keep fruit from turning brown.

SYRIA   # POTATO SALAD

SERVINGS: 4

TIME NEEDED: 30 minutes, plus boiling time

INGREDIENTS

1 lb potatoes	¼ tsp black pepper
1 Tb olive oil	1 Tb chopped parsley
juice of 1 large lemon	2 medium tomatoes, thinly
1 medium onion, chopped	sliced
1 tsp cold water	1 Tb dried mint
⅛ tsp salt	olives (optional)

EQUIPMENT

medium saucepan   medium bowl   juicer   chopper

PREPARATION

Boil   potatoes just until tender but still firm; then peel and cut
into 1-inch cubes.

Sprinkle oil over potatoes in bowl, stirring gently to coat each cube;
then add lemon juice and stir gently.

Add   onion, water, salt, and pepper to potatoes and stir lightly.

Garnish   with parsley, tomato slices, and mint.

Traditionally, olives are added as garnish. If your diet permits olives,
a low-salt variety can be used.

BENIN

SPICY SAUCE

SERVINGS: 18 (as sauce); 36 (as dip)
TIME NEEDED: 10 minutes, plus chilling time

INGREDIENTS

16 ozs tomato sauce
½ cup chopped onion
½ cup freshly squeezed lemon
  juice

1 Tb garlic powder
2–3 tsps crushed red pepper

EQUIPMENT

chopper   juicer   1-qt jar or bowl

PREPARATION

Combine   all ingredients (use 3 tsps red pepper for a "hotter" sauce)
          and mix thoroughly.
   Chill   in refrigerator until ready to serve.

BOTSWANA

CASHEW NUT SAUCE

SERVINGS: 6
TIME NEEDED: 25 minutes

INGREDIENTS

1½ tsps margarine
3 Tbs flour
1 cup finely chopped unsalted cashew nuts
pinch of sugar

1 cup unsalted beef stock, skimmed, or prepared bouillon
pinch of black pepper

EQUIPMENT

large skillet   chopper

PREPARATION

Melt   margarine in skillet and add flour, stirring until browned.
Add   cashew nuts and sugar; then add broth, a little at a time, stirring well to prevent lumps from forming.
Boil   5 minutes, skimming foam and fat from top of sauce; then add pepper.
Serve   hot with fish, rice, or yam dishes.

CYPRUS ## LEMON-MUSTARD SAUCE

SERVINGS: 8–10
TIME NEEDED: 10 minutes

INGREDIENTS

2 medium garlic cloves
4 Tbs lemon juice
2 Tbs wine vinegar
1 tsp dried mustard

⅛ tsp salt
⅛ tsp black pepper
½ cup olive oil

EQUIPMENT

small bowl   whisk   garlic press.   strainer   cruet or bottle with tight cap

PREPARATION

Crush   garlic in press.
Combine   lemon juice, vinegar, mustard, salt, and pepper in bowl; add oil gradually, beating with whisk until sauce thickens; then add crushed garlic.
Strain   sauce into cruet and refrigerate until ready to serve.
Serve   hot or cold, traditionally on fish, poultry, or meat dishes.

PANAMA **CHILI-MUSTARD DRESSING**

SERVINGS: 4–6
TIME NEEDED: 10 minutes, plus standing time

INGREDIENTS

1 medium onion, quartered
½ small green hot chili, seeded
  and chopped

½ cup white vinegar
1 tsp prepared mustard
1 bay leaf

EQUIPMENT

medium bowl   strainer   cruet or small pitcher

PREPARATION

Mix   all ingredients thoroughly in bowl.
Set aside   4 hours or longer.
Strain   into cruet or small pitcher for serving on bean or other cold vegetable salads.

PANAMA   # CRABMEAT DRESSING

SERVINGS: 8–12
TIME NEEDED: 10 minutes, plus chilling time

INGREDIENTS

1½ cups mayonnaise or salad
  dressing*
1 Tb lemon juice
1½ tsps paprika

6 ozs fresh or canned
  crabmeat, drained and
  shredded

EQUIPMENT

medium bowl

PREPARATION

Combine   all ingredients and blend well.
  Serve   chilled; keep refrigerated until ready to serve.

*For restricted diets, various low calorie, low-salt, and reduced-cholesterol products are now available, or if preferable, make dressing with half mayonnaise and half yogurt.

SYRIA   **EGGPLANT SAUCE**

SERVINGS: 16
TIME NEEDED: 30 minutes, plus draining and simmering time

INGREDIENTS

½ tsp salt
2 1½-lb eggplants, peeled and
  cut into small cubes
3 Tbs olive oil
2 large onions, finely chopped
2 tsps paprika

2 tsps dried savory
1 tsp ground cumin
1 tsp ground coriander
1 tsp sugar
32 ozs canned plum tomatoes

EQUIPMENT

chopper   colander   7-qt Dutch oven

PREPARATION

Sprinkle   salt over eggplant cubes in colander and toss well, let drain
           for 30 minutes; then squeeze moisture from eggplant until
           quite dry.
   Heat   oil in Dutch oven over moderate heat; cook onions until
           tender, add eggplant, and sauté until lightly browned.
    Add   paprika, savory, cumin, coriander, and sugar; cook 1 min-
           ute, stirring thoroughly; then add undrained tomatoes.
 Simmer   30 minutes, covered, on low heat.
  Serve   hot over meat loaf or cooked rice or grains.*

*Sauce will keep for a few days in refrigerator and may be reheated in
saucepan over moderate heat; or it can be frozen.

TURKEY   # YOGURT AND HONEY SAUCE

SERVINGS: 8–12*
TIME NEEDED: 10 minutes, plus chilling time

INGREDIENTS

1 cup plain yogurt   *1 tsp ground coriander*
2 Tbs honey   *1 tsp ground cumin*
⅛ tsp salt   *1 tsp ground cinnamon*
1 Tb paprika

EQUIPMENT

medium bowl

PREPARATION

Combine   all ingredients, blending thoroughly.
  Chill   in refrigerator, covered, until ready to serve.

*Servings vary depending on whether sauce is used as dip for crackers, toast rounds, etc., or if it is poured onto individual servings of fruit salad, cottage cheese salad, grilled chicken, or Turkish pastry.

ALBANIA
CHICKEN BARLEY SOUP
WITH YOGURT

SERVINGS: 6

TIME NEEDED: 60 minutes, plus simmering time

INGREDIENTS

2 Tbs pearl barley	1 egg
4 cups chicken broth, skimmed	2½ cups yogurt
¼ tsp black pepper	3 Tbs chopped parsley

EQUIPMENT

2-qt saucepan   chopper   medium bowl   wire wisk

PREPARATION

Combine barley, broth, and pepper in saucepan.

Heat to boiling over moderate heat; then lower heat.

Simmer 45 to 60 minutes, covered, or until barley is tender but not mushy.

Beat egg in bowl until well blended; add yogurt, blending well; then add ¼ cup hot soup to yogurt mixture, continuing to beat with whisk until smooth.

Add yogurt-egg mixture to soup, stirring to blend well; then add parsley.

Cook over very low heat, stirring occasionally, until mixture is heated through; do *not* allow soup to boil or yogurt may curdle.

Serve hot.

BAHAMAS   # OKRA SOUP

SERVINGS: 12

TIME NEEDED: 35 minutes, plus simmering time

INGREDIENTS

3 Tbs vegetable oil	1 bay leaf
2 medium onions, diced	2 qts water
1/3 cup diced celery stalks	1 lb potatoes, peeled and diced
1/4 lb carrots, pared and diced	1 lb lean tender lamb, cut into
1 lb okra, diced	small cubes
4 ozs tomato paste	1/8 tsp salt
1/8 tsp dried thyme	Tabasco sauce to taste

EQUIPMENT

large saucepan or Dutch oven

PREPARATION

Heat oil in saucepan over moderate heat; add onions and cook until soft; then add celery, carrots, and okra.

Cook 3 minutes; then add tomato paste, thyme, and bay leaf and cook 3 more minutes; then add water, potatoes, lamb, and salt.

Simmer 1½ hours, checking occasionally to see if any fat has risen to top to be skimmed off.

Serve hot, seasoned with Tabasco sauce.

THE BRITISH ISLES

CURRIED PARSNIP SOUP

SERVINGS: 8

TIME NEEDED: 45 minutes, plus simmering time

INGREDIENTS

3 Tbs margarine

1½ lbs parsnips, peeled and diced

1 cup chopped onions

2 garlic cloves, minced

2 Tbs flour

1 scant Tb curry powder

2 qts beef broth, skimmed

EQUIPMENT

heavy medium saucepan or 3-qt Dutch oven   chopper   whisk blender   large heat-resistant bowl

PREPARATION

Melt margarine in saucepan over low heat; add parsnips, onions, and garlic.

Cook 5 minutes, stirring occasionally; then add flour, stirring well, and curry powder.

Cook 1 minute; then add broth, heat to boiling over moderate heat; then lower heat.

Simmer 25 minutes, covered, or until parsnips are tender.

Pour 1–2 cups soup into blender. Do *not* fill more than one-third full, and make sure that soup is not too hot; otherwise container may explode; then transfer pureed soup to large bowl, repeating blending procedure until all soup has been pureed.

Reheat soup before serving.

BULGARIA   **COLD CUCUMBER SOUP**

SERVINGS: 6–8
TIME NEEDED: 30 minutes, plus chilling time

INGREDIENTS

light sprinkling of salt
1 large cucumber, peeled and diced
3 cups yogurt
¼ cup very finely chopped fresh mint

2 Tbs chopped currants
3 cloves, crushed
2 cups ice-cold water
1 Tb olive oil

EQUIPMENT

peeler   small bowl   chopper   large bowl   whisk

PREPARATION

Sprinkle   salt over cucumber in small bowl; then set aside for 10 minutes.

Wash   salt from cucumber and transfer to large bowl; then add yogurt, mint, currants, cloves, water, and oil.

Beat   with whisk until oil is completely mixed into soup.

Chill   thoroughly before serving.

COLOMBIA   # LIMA BEAN SOUP

SERVINGS: 6–8

TIME NEEDED: 45 minutes, plus simmering time

INGREDIENTS

1 large meaty soup bone,
  trimmed of fat
1 medium onion, chopped
1 large carrot, chopped
2 Tbs chopped parsley
1½ cups canned tomatoes

12 ozs frozen green baby lima
  beans
¼ cup cornstarch
⅓ cup milk
¼ tsp salt
¼ tsp black pepper

EQUIPMENT

chopper   large deep soup kettle   small dish   large slotted spoon

PREPARATION

Cover   soup bone in kettle with water and add onion, carrot, parsley, and canned tomatoes.

Heat   to boiling; then lower heat and simmer 2 hours, or until meat on bone is very tender.

Remove   bone with slotted spoon; cut meat from bone into small pieces and add to soup; discard bone; then add lima beans and simmer 20 minutes, or until beans are barely tender.

Blend   cornstarch with milk and a little hot soup in small dish until smooth; then add cornstarch mixture to soup in kettle, plus salt and pepper.

Simmer   10 to 15 minutes until flavors have blended well, and soup is slightly thick and completely rewarmed.

Serve   hot.

GRENADA　　　**TOMATO SOUP**

SERVINGS: 6–8
TIME NEEDED: 45 minutes, plus simmering time

INGREDIENTS

1 Tb margarine	½ tsp dried thyme
2 ozs lean ham, trimmed, shaved, or chipped, and chopped	¼ tsp ground mace
	6 sprigs parsley
	1 qt chicken broth, skimmed
2 medium onions, chopped	2 Tbs cornstarch or flour
1 small green pepper, chopped	2 Tbs water
2 lbs tomatoes, quartered	¼ tsp grated nutmeg

EQUIPMENT

chopper　　4-qt Dutch oven　　mill or blender　　medium bowl
small bowl　　grater

PREPARATION

Melt　　margarine in Dutch oven over moderate heat; add ham, onions, and green pepper, stirring well.

Cook　　5 minutes, stirring occasionally; add tomatoes and cook 5 more minutes; then add thyme, mace, parsley, and chicken broth.

Heat　　to boiling, then reduce heat to low and simmer 30 to 40 minutes, covered, or until tomatoes are completely softened.

Puree　　soup through mill or blender. Do *not* fill blender more than one-third of the way, and make sure that soup is not too hot; otherwise container may explode. Transfer each portion of blended soup to medium bowl until all soup has been processed; then return soup to Dutch oven.

Blend　　cornstarch and water in small bowl to make smooth paste and add to soup, blending thoroughly; then heat soup to boiling over moderate heat, stirring constantly, until it begins to thicken; then lower heat.

Simmer　　5 minutes, uncovered, and add nutmeg.
Serve　　hot.

GUATEMALA   **CARROT SOUP**

SERVINGS: 8

TIME NEEDED: 30 minutes, plus boiling and simmering time

INGREDIENTS

1½ lbs trimmed soup bones,
  preferably beef
1 medium onion, sliced
2 celery stalks with leaves, cut
  into 1-inch pieces
¼ large green pepper, sliced
  into thin strips
1 garlic clove, chopped
8 large pared carrots, cut into
  thirds

1½ qts water
¼ tsp salt
1 Tb margarine
¼ cup chopped onion
¼ cup grated low-salt
  Parmesan-type cheese
  (optional)

EQUIPMENT

4-qt soup pot or Dutch oven   chopper   parer
large heat-resistant bowl   blender   10-inch skillet

PREPARATION

Combine   all ingredients except margarine, chopped onion, and
  cheese in soup pot.

Heat   to boiling over moderate heat; then reduce to low heat.

Simmer   1 hour.

Remove   bones from soup, skim off fat and particles that have risen
  to top; then puree a small amount in blender. Do *not* fill
  more than one-third of the way, and make sure that soup
  is not too hot; otherwise container may explode.

Transfer   pureed soup to bowl and repeat procedure with rest of
  soup and vegetables.

Melt   margarine in skillet and cook chopped onion about 5 minutes, until tender; do not brown.

Return   pureed soup to large pot, stir cooked onion and cheese
  into soup.

Warm   5 minutes over moderate heat, or until completely hot.

MONGOLIA   # NOODLE SOUP WITH DRIED BEEF*

SERVINGS: 8
TIME NEEDED: 45 minutes, plus baking, standing, and simmering time

INGREDIENTS

½ lb lean round steak,
   trimmed and thinly sliced
2 qts water
2 Tbs margarine
2 medium onions, chopped
2 garlic cloves, minced

¼ tsp salt
¼ tsp black pepper
1 cup uncooked thin egg
   noodles, or egg-free or
   transparent noodles

EQUIPMENT

jelly-roll pan or baking sheet   grinder or processor   3-qt saucepan
or soup pot   chopper   10-inch skillet

PREPARATION

Preheat oven to lowest possible setting.

Bake steak strips in single layer on baking sheet about 1 hour, or until meat is dry, turning slices occasionally to dry well on both sides; then remove and let cool.

Grind meat, using fine blade.

Heat water in saucepan over moderate heat until boiling; then add meat, remove from heat, and let stand 10 minutes, covered.

Melt margarine in skillet over low heat, add onions and garlic, and cook until tender; then add salt and pepper.

Combine onion-garlic mixture with soup and heat to boiling; then reduce to low heat.

Simmer 20 minutes, covered; then add noodles and simmer 6 to 8 minutes, or until noodles are soft.

---

*In Mongolia, dried meat is made by hanging slices on string to dry, generally during the cold time of year. This process preserves much nutritive value and provides a staple, indispensable food for travelers since it is not quickly perishable and can be easily reconstituted in various ways, such as Mongolian "borts," or chunks.

PARAGUAY **SQUASH AND CHEESE SOUP**

SERVINGS: 6–8
TIME NEEDED: 30 minutes, plus simmering time

INGREDIENTS

2 Tbs margarine
2 cups coarsely grated acorn
  squash
½ cup grated onion
1 Tb flour
¼ cup grated Parmesan-type
  cheese*

1½ qts chicken or beef broth,
  skimmed
¼ cup finely diced Monterey
  Jack cheese*
1 heaping Tb chopped parsley

EQUIPMENT

grater or processor   4-qt Dutch oven   wire whisk   chopper
soup tureen or large serving bowl

PREPARATION

Melt   margarine in Dutch oven over low heat and add squash
        and onions.

Cook   5 minutes, stirring occasionally, or until vegetables are
        tender; then stir flour into vegetable mixture and cook 1 to
        2 minutes, stirring constantly.

Add   grated cheese, blending well; then gradually add broth,
        stirring continuously with whisk.

Cook   over moderate heat until soup boils; then lower heat and
        simmer 10 minutes, stirring occasionally.

Scatter diced cheese on bottom of tureen and pour hot soup over
        cheese.

Garnish with parsley and serve hot.

*Several types of low-salt cheeses are now available. To make a "creamed" version of this soup, use 1 quart water plus 2 cups milk in place of broth.

SWEDEN   # SPRING SOUP

SERVINGS: 8–10
TIME NEEDED: 30 minutes, plus simmering time

INGREDIENTS

3 Tbs margarine
6 large carrots, scraped and
  sliced
¼ lb small leeks, sliced
½ lb fresh spinach, destemmed
  and chopped
1 small bunch radishes (8–12),
  sliced

4 Tbs flour
2 qts chicken broth, skimmed
⅛ tsp black pepper
2 egg yolks
½ cup half-and-half, light
  cream, or yogurt

EQUIPMENT

scraper   chopper   3-qt saucepan   whisk   small bowl

PREPARATION

Melt margarine in saucepan over moderate heat; add carrots and leeks, cook until tender, stirring occasionally; then add spinach and cook until wilted.

Add radishes and flour, blending thoroughly; then cook 2 minutes over low heat, stirring constantly.

Add chicken broth gradually, stirring well; heat soup to boiling; then lower heat.

Simmer 10 minutes, covered, or until vegetables are tender; then add pepper.

Beat egg yolks in bowl with half-and half until well blended; then pour slowly into hot soup over low heat, beating briskly with whisk; do *not* let soup boil or egg-cream mixture may curdle.

Serve hot.

Traditionally this soup is made with heavy cream.

UNITED STATES ## BEAN SOUP

SERVINGS: 8–12

TIME NEEDED: 60 minutes, plus soaking and simmering time

INGREDIENTS

1¼ lbs pea beans (navy beans)
2 qts water
6 cups water
1 ham or veal soup bone
½ tsp salt
½ tsp black pepper
1 lb potatoes, peeled

3 medium onions, chopped
2 celery stalks, chopped
1 Tb chopped parsley
1 garlic clove, minced
pinch of chopped chili for each
   serving (optional)

EQUIPMENT

large Dutch oven or heavy soup pot   peeler   small saucepan
chopper   masher or ricer

PREPARATION

Rinse   beans well and remove those of poor quality.

Heat   2 quarts water in Dutch oven until boiling vigorously; then add beans slowly and boil 4 minutes.

Remove   pot from heat and soak beans 1 hour in hot water, covered.

Add   6 cups water, soup bone, salt, and pepper.

Simmer   2 hours over low flame, covered, stirring occasionally to keep beans from sticking.

Boil   potatoes in saucepan about 20 minutes, or until soft enough to be easily mashed or put through ricer.

Add   onions, celery, parsley, garlic, and mashed potatoes to soup; mix well.

Simmer   1 hour, covered; remove bone from soup, skim fat and foam from top.

Serve   hot.*

*For a spicier soup, sprinkle a pinch of chopped chili on top of each serving.

UNITED STATES **SQUASH SOUP**

SERVINGS: 6–8
TIME NEEDED: 30 minutes, plus simmering time

INGREDIENTS

2 Tbs margarine
4 medium onions, chopped
1 cup chopped celery stalks
   and leaves
1 small garlic clove, minced
1 qt chicken broth, skimmed
2 cups mashed cooked squash*
½ tsp dried rosemary†

½ tsp dried savory†
¼ tsp dried tarragon†
1 heaping Tb chopped fresh
   parsley
1 cup yogurt
pinch of salt
⅛ tsp white pepper
pinch of nutmeg per serving

EQUIPMENT

chopper   medium saucepan   small bowl

PREPARATION

Melt margarine in saucepan over moderate heat and sauté onions, celery, and garlic until soft and golden; then add broth, squash, rosemary, savory, tarragon, and parsley.

Heat to boiling; then lower heat and simmer 15 minutes.

Pour yogurt into bowl, adding ½ cup soup gradually, stirring well; then return mixture to soup in saucepan, pouring slowly and stirring well; do *not* let soup boil or yogurt may curdle.

Add salt and pepper.

Sprinkle nutmeg over each serving of hot soup.

---

*Use a firm squash, such as acorn squash or any other winter squash.
†If fresh herbs are used, double the amount.

BARBADOS ## DOVED PEAS

SERVINGS: 6–8
TIME NEEDED: 30 minutes

INGREDIENTS

2 cups water
1¼ lbs fresh or frozen green
  peas
2 Tbs olive oil
4 medium onions, finely
  chopped

¼ tsp cayenne pepper*
½ tsp dried marjoram
pinch of salt

EQUIPMENT

4-qt saucepan   strainer   chopper   4-qt Dutch oven

PREPARATION

Boil   water in saucepan; then lower heat, add peas, and simmer 5 minutes, or until peas are cooked.
Drain   peas and set aside.
Heat   oil in Dutch oven; add onions and cook 5 minutes, or until tender, stirring occasionally.
Combine   cooked peas with onions, plus pepper, marjoram, and salt.
Cook   5 minutes, stirring occasionally.
Serve   hot.

Customarily this dish is made with 6 slices bacon diced, cooked in Dutch oven until light brown, and left in pan to be mixed with onions while they brown. If so desired, this recipe can be made with turkey bacon or one of the new brands of bacon made with reduced salt.

*For a less spicy dish, halve the cayenne pepper.

GERMANY   **BEETS IN SPICED SAUCE**

SERVINGS: 6–8
TIME NEEDED: 30 minutes, plus simmering time

INGREDIENTS

3 Tbs margarine
1 small onion, very finely
   chopped
2 Tbs flour
1 cup low-salt beef broth,
   skimmed
¼ cup red wine vinegar

½ tsp caraway seeds
⅛ tsp ground cloves
¼ cup sugar
2 Tbs prepared horseradish
2 lbs beets, canned or fresh
   cooked, sliced and drained
3 Tbs yogurt

EQUIPMENT

colander   2-qt saucepan   chopper   wire whisk

PREPARATION

Melt   margarine in saucepan over moderate heat; add onion and
cook until tender; then blend in flour until smooth and cook
1 minute, stirring well.

Add   broth gradually, stirring constantly until mixture begins to
boil and thicken; then stir in vinegar, caraway seeds,
cloves, sugar, and horseradish.

Simmer   5 minutes over low heat; then add beets, blending thoroughly, and cook 5 to 10 minutes, or until completely
heated.

Stir   yogurt into mixture and cook 2 minutes over very low
flame; do *not* boil or yogurt may curdle.

The traditional version of this dish is richer because it uses sour cream
instead of yogurt.

GREECE

ARTICHOKES WITH
LEMON SAUCE

SERVINGS: 6
TIME NEEDED: 25 minutes, plus simmering time

INGREDIENTS

1 cup chicken broth, skimmed
9 ozs frozen artichoke hearts
1 tsp cornstarch
2 tsps water
2 eggs

3 Tbs lemon juice
¼ cup chopped parsley
⅛ tsp freshly ground black
   pepper

EQUIPMENT

2-qt saucepan   small dish   whisk or beater   small bowl   chopper
pepper mill

PREPARATION

Boil   chicken broth in saucepan over moderate heat; add artichoke hearts and cook 5 minutes, or until tender.

Stir   cornstarch and water in dish to form smooth paste; then
add to hot broth, stirring well.

Heat   to boiling, stirring constantly until mixture thickens slightly
and liquid is clear.

Beat   eggs and lemon juice in bowl very well; add a little hot
liquid to egg mixture, beating continuously until smooth;
then pour egg mixture into liquid in saucepan, over very
low heat, beating until well blended.

Simmer   3 to 5 minutes, or until sauce thickens, stirring lightly; do
not boil or eggs will curdle.

Add   parsley and pepper.

Serve   hot.

HUNGARY **KOHLRABI WITH GREEN PEAS**

SERVINGS: 6–8
TIME NEEDED: 30 minutes

INGREDIENTS

2 cups water
8 small-to-medium tender
  kohlrabi, peeled, destemmed
  and thinly sliced
2 Tbs margarine
1½ Tbs flour

1 lb fresh green peas, shelled,
  or 12 ozs frozen
pinch of salt
⅛ tsp black pepper
1 Tb very finely chopped
  parsley

EQUIPMENT

peeler   medium saucepan   colander or strainer   container for
hot liquid

PREPARATION

Heat   water to boiling over moderate heat and cook kohlrabi 5
        minutes, or until barely tender; then drain and set aside,
        saving liquid in container.

Melt   margarine in saucepan and add flour, blending thoroughly,
        plus 1 cup reserved liquid, stirring until smooth and thick-
        ened; then add peas.

Simmer 5 to 10 minutes, stirring occasionally, or until peas are just
        tender.

Stir   cooked kohlrabi, salt, pepper, and parsley into mixture.

Simmer 2 minutes over very low flame, or until heated through.

JAMAICA **SWEET POTATO PUDDING**

SERVINGS: 6
TIME NEEDED: 20 minutes, plus baking time

INGREDIENTS

1 lb sweet potatoes, peeled
¼ cup margarine
½ cup brown sugar
¼ cup flour
¼ tsp ground nutmeg

¼ tsp ground ginger
1 cup milk
½ tsp vanilla extract
½ cup raisins

EQUIPMENT

grater sifter medium bowl medium pudding or baking dish, oiled or nonstick

PREPARATION

Preheat oven to 375°F.
Grate sweet potatoes into bowl; add margarine and brown sugar.
Sift flour, nutmeg, and ginger; then combine with potato mixture.
Add milk slowly, mixing well; then add vanilla and raisins.
Bake 1½ hours in baking dish, or until pudding is firm to the touch.
Serve hot or cold.

Traditionally this is a much richer pudding because recipe calls for coconut milk.

NEPAL   ## SPICED POTATOES

SERVINGS: 6–8
TIME NEEDED: 20 minutes, plus boiling time

INGREDIENTS

2 lbs potatoes, unpeeled   ¼ cup lemon juice
¼ cup olive oil   2 Tbs chopped hot green or
2 Tbs dry mustard   red pepper
⅛ tsp salt

EQUIPMENT

medium saucepan   medium bowl   small bowl   chopper

PREPARATION

Cover   potatoes with water in saucepan and boil 20 to 30 min-
          utes, or until tender but still firm.
Peel   potatoes, cut into 1-inch cubes, and hold in medium bowl.
Combine   oil, mustard, salt, and lemon juice in small bowl, mix well,
          and pour over potato cubes.
Toss   lightly but thoroughly to coat all cubes with seasoning.
Sprinkle hot pepper over potatoes, and toss lightly before serving.

TANZANIA   # POTATO DELIGHT

SERVINGS: 6
TIME NEEDED: 45 minutes, plus simmering time

INGREDIENTS

1½ lbs potatoes, peeled
2 Tbs vegetable oil
1 large onion, thinly sliced
2 tomatoes, peeled and thinly
  sliced
½ cup unsalted peanuts

⅛ tsp salt
1 tsp curry powder
½ cup canned unseasoned
  pumpkin*
½ cup water

EQUIPMENT

3-qt saucepan   masher   12-inch skillet

PREPARATION

Cover   potatoes in saucepan with water, bring to a boil over moderate heat; then lower heat.

Simmer   20 minutes, covered, or until potatoes are tender; then mash coarsely and set aside.

Heat   oil in skillet over moderate heat, add onion, and cook until tender; do not brown; then add tomatoes, peanuts, salt, and curry powder.

Cook   3 minutes, stirring occasionally; add potatoes and pumpkin and cook 2 more minutes, blending thoroughly.

Add   water and blend very well.

Simmer   5 minutes, or until completely heated.

*Use only plain canned or fresh homemade pumpkin. Do not use canned pumpkin-pie filling, which comes already seasoned.

ZAMBIA   # VEGETABLE STEW

SERVINGS: 4–6
TIME NEEDED: 25 minutes, plus simmering time

INGREDIENTS

2 Tbs vegetable oil
1 large onion, diced
½ lb squash, peeled and sliced
½ lb cabbage, quartered and sliced into strips
½ lb cauliflower florets, sliced
½ lb potatoes, peeled and cut into sixths

1 cup fresh or frozen green peas
1 cup water
½ bouillon cube*
½ tsp sage
¼ tsp black pepper

EQUIPMENT

peeler   chopper   12-inch saucepan with tight cover

PREPARATION

Combine   oil and onion in saucepan and sauté on low heat until limp; do not brown; then add squash, cabbage, cauliflower, potatoes, and peas and sauté on low heat until oil is absorbed.

Add   water, mixing well, plus halved bouillon cube, sage, and pepper.

Simmer   30 minutes, covered, on very low heat, until vegetables are tender, but check to be sure they do not get mushy.

*Beef bouillon cubes are usually quite salty. For strict salt reduction, use bouillon granules, which may often contain less salt. Or, use homemade beef (or chicken) broth prepared without added salt and with fat skimmed off the top. Use about ½ cup broth and reduce the amount of water to about ½ cup.

Entrées
Fish and Seafood

SPICY FISH

SERVINGS: 6

TIME NEEDED: 35 minutes, plus simmering time

INGREDIENTS

¼ tsp salt

4 Tbs flour

1½ lbs sea bass, cod, haddock, or perch, sliced into serving portions

¼–⅓ cup vegetable oil for frying

1 medium onion, coarsely chopped

1½ cups tomato sauce

¾ cup water

½ tsp cayenne pepper

2 bay leaves

EQUIPMENT

chopper   10-inch skillet   paper towels   large platter

PREPARATION

Sprinkle salt and flour over fish, making sure to coat each piece well.

Heat enough oil in skillet, until haze forms over oil, to allow quick deep-frying over moderate flame.

Fry fish portions until brown on both sides.

Drain fish on paper towels on platter.

Pour out all but 2 Tbs hot oil from skillet; add onion and cook over moderate heat until lightly browned.

Add tomato sauce, water, pepper, and bay leaves and heat to boiling; then lower heat.

Simmer 5 minutes; then return fish to sauce in skillet.

Simmer 10 minutes, uncovered, or until fish flakes easily.

Traditionally served with rice or plantains.

CYPRUS   **GRILLED MARINATED FISH**

SERVINGS: 6
TIME NEEDED: 15 minutes, plus marinating and broiling time

INGREDIENTS

⅓ cup white vinegar
⅛ tsp salt
⅛ tsp cayenne pepper
⅓ cup olive oil

1 medium onion, thinly sliced
6 portions ocean perch,
   whiting, or haddock

EQUIPMENT

large shallow baking dish   medium bowl   whisk

PREPARATION

Combine vinegar, salt, pepper, and oil in bowl, blending thoroughly with whisk; then add onion.

Place fish portions in baking dish large enough to hold them without overlapping; cover each slice with marinade and onion slices.

Marinate 3 to 4 hours, covered, in refrigerator, turning fish occasionally to marinate on both sides.

Preheat broiler.

Broil fish 4 inches from heat source, turning once; cook until skin becomes golden brown and "bubbly," and fish flakes easily.

Traditionally served with a Lemon-Mustard Sauce (page 222).

EL SALVADOR   **BAKED HADDOCK**

SERVINGS: 6

TIME NEEDED: 30 minutes, plus standing and baking time

INGREDIENTS

3–4-lb haddock, red snapper,   3 large onions, sliced
  or pollock, cleaned   5 large tomatoes, peeled and
¼ tsp salt   sliced
½ tsp black pepper   ¼ cup chopped parsley
4 Tbs lemon juice   2 Tbs olive oil
2 medium garlic cloves,
  crushed

EQUIPMENT

shallow 3-qt baking dish or large casserole, nonstick or lightly
greased   garlic press   chopper   aluminum foil

PREPARATION

Preheat   oven to 350°F.

Rub   fish with salt, ¼ tsp pepper, and 1 Tb lemon juice; then
spread with garlic.

Let stand   15 minutes in covered baking dish.

Cover   fish with half of sliced onions, sprinkle ⅛ tsp pepper on
onion slices; then add half the tomato slices.

Sprinkle   remaining pepper on mixture, plus half the parsley.

Repeat   layering rest of ingredients, finishing with parsley on top;
then pour 3 Tbs lemon juice over layers, plus oil.

Cover   with aluminum foil.

Bake   30 minutes, covered; then 20 minutes, uncovered, or
until fish flakes easily.

FRANCE   **FISH FILLET WITH
                          GREEN GRAPES**

SERVINGS: 6
TIME NEEDED: 45 minutes

INGREDIENTS

¼ tsp salt	½ tsp paprika
2½ lbs fillet of sole, flounder, or fluke	⅛ tsp white pepper
	juice of 1 lemon
2 Tbs margarine	½ cup water
¼ cup dry white wine	½ lb seedless green grapes

EQUIPMENT

small saucepan   10-inch skillet   juicer   slotted spatula
slotted spoon   heatproof platter

PREPARATION

Sprinkle   salt lightly over fish, and gently fold each portion in half.
Heat   margarine in skillet over moderate heat, distribute folded fish in skillet; then sauté 1 minute on each side.
Pour   wine over fish; then sprinkle with paprika and pepper.
Dilute   lemon juice with water and pour over fish, cook over moderate heat until sauce boils; then lower heat.
Simmer   3 to 5 minutes, or until fish flakes easily; then remove fish with slotted spatula to platter; keep warm.
Add   grapes to skillet; reheat until sauce boils; then reduce heat.
Simmer   2 minutes, uncovered.
Remove   grapes with slotted spoon, and serve with fish fillets.

LUXEMBOURG ## BRAISED FISH

SERVINGS: 6

TIME NEEDED: 45 minutes, plus baking time

INGREDIENTS

2 Tbs margarine	*1 cup dry white wine*
4 medium onions, chopped	*1 Tb flour*
¼ cup chopped parsley	*¼ cup yogurt*
⅛ tsp salt	*1 tsp prepared mustard*
¼ tsp black peppercorns	
6 fillets of small whole trout,	
red snapper, or bass	

EQUIPMENT

chopper   4-quart Dutch oven   large shallow baking dish
small dish or bowl

PREPARATION

Preheat   oven to 350°F.

Melt   margarine in Dutch oven over low heat, add onions, parsley, salt, and peppercorns; cook until onions are soft; then remove from heat.

Arrange   fish in Dutch oven, and cover with wine.

Bake   20 minutes, covered, or until fish flakes easily.

Lower   oven to 200°F.

Transfer   fish to baking dish, cover, and keep warm in oven.

Blend   flour, yogurt, and mustard in dish to make smooth paste; then stir into wine sauce remaining in Dutch oven, and heat over moderate heat, stirring to keep smooth; do not boil.

Serve   fish warm with sauce poured over it.

This dish is customarily made with heavy cream, and a half slice of thick bacon is either inserted into the whole fish, or laid on top of each portion before baking.

PAKISTAN   **SHRIMP CURRY**

SERVINGS: 6–8

TIME NEEDED: 30 minutes, plus simmering time

INGREDIENTS

1 pint yogurt

2 large garlic cloves, minced

2 medium onions, finely ground

4 medium tomatoes, chopped

1 small bunch fresh coriander, chopped, or ½ tsp ground coriander

½ tsp cayenne pepper, or ground hot red pepper

2 tsps ground turmeric

1 tsp fresh ground ginger, or 1 Tb dried ground ginger

⅛ tsp salt

1 Tb vegetable oil

1 tsp dill seeds

2 lbs raw medium shrimp, peeled and cleaned

EQUIPMENT

large bowl   grinder or processor   chopper   12-inch skillet

PREPARATION

Combine   yogurt, garlic, onions, tomatoes, coriander, pepper, turmeric, ginger, and salt in bowl.

Heat   oil in skillet over moderate heat, and add dill seeds, cooking until lightly browned; then lower heat, and add seasoned yogurt mixture.

Simmer   5 minutes; then add shrimp and simmer 10 minutes, or until shrimp turn pink and are cooked.

SRI LANKA   # MACKEREL CURRY

SERVINGS: 8–10
TIME NEEDED: 30 minutes, plus simmering time

INGREDIENTS

4 lbs mackerel, sliced into
  serving portions
½ tsp salt
1 Tb chili powder
2 Tbs vegetable oil

2 large onions, chopped
2 tsps dill seeds
6 medium garlic cloves, minced
2 lbs tomatoes, chopped
½ tsp turmeric

EQUIPMENT

chopper   12-inch skillet

PREPARATION

Sprinkle both sides of fish slices with salt and half the chili powder.
Heat oil in skillet over moderate heat and cook onions until slightly browned, stirring occasionally.
Add dill seeds, garlic, tomatoes, turmeric, and remaining chili powder.
Simmer 5 minutes on low heat; then add seasoned fish slices.
Simmer 10 minutes, covered, or until fish flakes easily; shake pan occasionally to "jiggle" pieces of fish to prevent sticking.

UNITED STATES   # BAKED FISH
STEAKS

SERVINGS: 6
TIME NEEDED: 15 minutes, plus baking time

INGREDIENTS

⅛ tsp salt
2 tsps crushed dill seeds
⅛ tsp cayenne pepper
6 steaks of salmon, halibut, or
    tuna
juice of 1 freshly squeezed
    lemon

3 Tbs herbed oil-vinegar salad
    dressing
1 cup yogurt
6 dashes of paprika
6 sprigs parsley

EQUIPMENT

small dish   large shallow baking pan, nonstick or lightly greased
juicer

PREPARATION

Preheat   oven to 350°F.
Combine   salt, dill, and pepper in dish, and sprinkle fish steaks on
           both sides with seasoning mixture; then arrange in baking
           pan without pieces overlapping.
Mix   lemon juice and salad dressing, and pour evenly over fish;
           then cover fish with yogurt.
Bake   45 to 60 minutes, until fish flakes easily and all pieces are
           cooked.
Garnish   each steak with paprika and parsley.

BOLIVIA ## CHICKEN WITH HOT PEPPER

SERVINGS: 6
TIME NEEDED: 45 minutes, plus simmering time

INGREDIENTS

1 stewing chicken, about 4 lbs	*¼ tsp black pepper*
2 carrots, scraped and cut into thirds	*2 Tbs vegetable oil*
1 celery stalk, halved	*1 medium onion, chopped finely*
1 medium onion, halved	*1 Tb cayenne pepper**
¼ tsp salt	*¼ oz unsweetened chocolate†*

EQUIPMENT

large saucepan or Dutch oven   chopper   large skillet

PREPARATION

Cover   chicken with water in saucepan, add carrots, celery, halved onion, salt, and black pepper; then heat to boiling over moderate heat.

Simmer   1 hour, covered, on low heat, or until chicken is tender; then remove chicken from broth and let cool.

Measure   2 cups broth and set aside.

Cut   large pieces of chicken from the bones, but do *not* use skin.

Heat   oil in skillet over moderate heat, cook chopped onion until tender; then mix cayenne pepper with onion.

Cook   1 minute, then gradually stir in premeasured chicken broth, chocolate, and chicken portions.

Simmer   10 to 15 minutes, covered, over low heat.

Serve   hot.

This Aymaran dish of the Bolivian Indians is customarily served with boiled potatoes.

*For a less spicy dish, add only 1 tsp cayenne pepper.
†You may substitute 1 tsp carob.

ITALY   **CHICKEN WITH MUSHROOMS**

SERVINGS: 6–8
TIME NEEDED: 45 minutes, plus simmering time

INGREDIENTS

3 Tbs olive oil
⅛ tsp salt
1 large garlic clove
2 large fresh basil leaves
1 tsp fresh, or ½ tsp dried,
  thyme
pinch of dried oregano

2 broiling chickens, 2–3 lbs
  each, split into halves
½ lb mushrooms, sliced
2 Tbs tomato paste
strained juice of 1 large lemon
¾ cup chicken stock

EQUIPMENT

7-qt Dutch oven   platter   juicer   small strainer

PREPARATION

Heat   oil in Dutch oven over moderate heat; then add salt, garlic, basil, thyme, oregano, and chicken halves, stirring well.

Sauté   chicken, turning all pieces until well browned; then remove and set aside on platter.

Discard   all but 2 Tbs oil from pan; then add mushrooms and sauté 2 minutes, stirring to cook evenly.

Add   tomato paste, mixing well, plus lemon juice, chicken stock, and sautéed chicken.

Simmer   20 minutes, covered, over low heat, or until chicken is tender.

JAPAN   # CHICKEN TERIYAKI

SERVINGS: 6–8

TIME NEEDED: 45 minutes, plus marinating time

INGREDIENTS

3 large whole chicken breasts,
totaling about 1½ lbs
2–2½ tsps freshly squeezed
ginger juice
3 Tbs Japanese soy sauce,
preferably low-salt variety

2 Tbs dry sherry or Japanese
sake
1 Tb cornstarch
2 Tbs vegetable oil

EQUIPMENT

large shallow dish for marinating   small bowl   garlic press
paper towels   12-inch skillet   very sharp slicing knife

PREPARATION

Arrange   chicken breasts in marinating dish.

Combine   ginger juice, soy sauce, and sherry in bowl and pour over
chicken.

Marinate   30 minutes; drain chicken, dry with paper towels; then
dust with cornstarch, saving marinade.

Heat   oil in skillet over moderate heat; cook chicken breasts
until brown on both sides; then pour reserved marinade
over chicken.

Cook   5 minutes, or until chicken is tender but firm; then slice
chicken breasts very thinly.

The chicken slices are usually served with thin slices or thin sticks of
raw vegetables, such as tomatoes, celery, cucumbers, or radishes.

MALAYSIA   # BAKED BARBECUED CHICKEN

SERVINGS: 8
TIME NEEDED: 30 minutes, plus marinating and baking time

INGREDIENTS

3 Tbs ground ginger, or a thin
  2-inch piece, freshly ground
⅓ cup soy sauce, preferably
  low-salt variety
2 Tbs vinegar

2 Tbs sugar
⅛ tsp black pepper
8 chicken thighs and 8
  drumsticks

EQUIPMENT

medium bowl   jelly-roll pan or baking pan

PREPARATION

Combine   ginger, soy sauce, vinegar, sugar, and pepper in bowl; then add chicken.

Marinate 2 hours, covered, at room temperature, or overnight in refrigerator, turning pieces occasionally to make sure they are evenly coated with seasoning.

Preheat   oven to 375°F.

Arrange   marinated chicken in baking pan.

Bake   1 hour, basting occasionally with marinade liquid, and turning pieces over at least once.

SAUDI ARABIA **CHICKEN IN BAKED APPLES**

SERVINGS: 6
TIME NEEDED: 30 minutes, plus baking time

INGREDIENTS

1 cup chopped cooked chicken
¼ tsp ground cloves
6 large baking apples, or firm cooking apples, washed, cored, unpeeled
1 Tb sugar
½ cup bread crumbs
2 Tbs margarine

EQUIPMENT

corer   chopper or processor   large baking dish or casserole
small saucepan

PREPARATION

Preheat   oven to 375°F.
Mix   chicken with cloves.
Fill   apple cavities with chicken, dividing evenly, and place apples in baking dish; add water to fill dish or pan about ¼ inch deep.
Sprinkle   ½ tsp sugar on top of each apple, and add bread crumbs, dividing evenly among all the apples.
Melt   margarine; then sprinkle on bread crumbs, dividing evenly among all the apples.
Bake   45 minutes, covered, or until apples are tender.
Bake   5 minutes more, uncovered, or until bread crumbs turn light brown.

TANZANIA   **CHICKEN CURRY**

SERVINGS: 6–8
TIME NEEDED: 60 minutes, plus simmering time

INGREDIENTS

2 3-lb chickens, cut into
  serving portions
⅛ tsp salt
½ tsp ground ginger
2 garlic cloves, minced
1 cup water
4 medium potatoes, peeled and
  halved

4 green chilis, 2 inches long,
  minced
½ tsp turmeric
½ tsp chili powder
2 medium green tomatoes,
  finely sliced
2 cups water

EQUIPMENT

4-qt Dutch oven   7-qt Dutch oven   slotted spoon   peeler

PREPARATION

Combine   chicken, salt, ginger, garlic, and 1 cup water in 4-qt Dutch oven, and heat to boiling; then lower heat.

Simmer   30 minutes, covered; then remove chicken with slotted spoon and set aside.

Boil   potatoes in liquid remaining in Dutch oven.

Combine   chilis, turmeric, chili powder, tomatoes, and 2 cups water in 7-qt Dutch oven.

Heat   to boiling over moderate heat, add chicken pieces, lower heat and simmer 30 minutes, covered, or until chicken is tender; then add boiled potatoes.

Simmer   5 to 10 minutes, uncovered, until liquid is reduced and potatoes are heated through.

Some diets do not allow coconut because of its high saturated fat content. However, traditionally this dish calls for canned shredded coconut (about 7 ozs) boiled in 2–3 cups water. After standing, the shredded coconut is discarded and only the coconut "milk" is used in place of water to finish cooking the chicken.

This dish is customarily made with hard-boiled eggs (4 per chicken). If your diet permits, add them along with boiled potatoes before final simmering.

UNITED STATES   POT ROASTED DUCK

SERVINGS: 6
TIME NEEDED: 30 minutes, plus simmering time

INGREDIENTS

⅛ tsp salt
¼ tsp black pepper
1 4–5-lb duck, trimmed and
   well washed
2 Tbs olive oil
2 cups hot water
pinch of fennel seeds

1 Tb crushed rosemary
1 cup chopped onions
1 cup chopped celery stalks
1 cup chopped carrots
1 parsnip, chopped
1 Tb chopped parsley

EQUIPMENT

large Dutch oven   chopper or processor   rack   platter

PREPARATION

Sprinkle   salt and pepper lightly over duck.
Heat   oil in Dutch oven over high heat and brown duck all over;
     then lower heat.
Add   water and all remaining ingredients.
Simmer   1½ to 2 hours, covered, or until duck is tender.
Set   duck on rack over platter to let fat drip off.
Serve   hot or cold.

SPICY GROUND BEEF

SERVINGS: 6–8
TIME NEEDED: 30 minutes, plus simmering time

INGREDIENTS

8 medium potatoes
1 Tb peanut oil
1 large onion, very finely
  chopped
3 Tbs paprika
½ tsp cayenne pepper

½ tsp ground cumin
1½ lbs lean, ground beef
1½ cups beef broth, skimmed
1½ cups green peas, fresh,
  canned, or frozen
⅛ tsp salt

EQUIPMENT

large saucepan   chopper   large Dutch oven

PREPARATION

Boil   potatoes in their jackets in saucepan.

Heat   oil in Dutch oven over moderate heat, add onion, and cook until lightly browned; add paprika, cayenne pepper, and cumin, blending well, cook 1 minute, stirring constantly; then mix in ground beef, and cook until meat is no longer pink.

Add   beef broth, green peas, and salt, and heat mixture to boiling; then lower heat.

Simmer   5 to 10 minutes,* uncovered, or until peas are cooked; if using fresh or frozen peas, add a little more beef broth if mixture dries out, since it should be juicy when served.

Peel   boiled potatoes and cut into quarters.

Serve   hot, with meat and peas covering potatoes.

*If drained, canned peas are used, the simmering time is generally only 5 minutes.

BOTSWANA # BAKED BEEF CUBES*

SERVINGS: 6
TIME NEEDED: 15 minutes, plus baking time

INGREDIENTS

⅛ tsp salt   *3 cups yogurt†*
2 lbs lean boneless beef,
  trimmed and cut into
  1½-inch squares

EQUIPMENT

3-qt Dutch oven

PREPARATION

Preheat   oven to 450°F.
Sprinkle salt lightly over meat in Dutch oven.
Spread   yogurt over meat, covering completely.
Bake   1 to 1½ hours, uncovered, or until top is slightly browned
            and meat is done.

*This dish is also called Lazy Granny.
†A traditional, richer version is made with sour cream.

BULGARIA   **BEEF STEW**

SERVINGS: 6–8
TIME NEEDED: 30 minutes, plus simmering time

INGREDIENTS

1 Tb vegetable oil

2 lbs lean boneless beef, cut
  into 1-inch cubes

1 Tb flour

1 Tb paprika

¼ tsp black pepper

1 bay leaf

½ cup red wine (optional)

1 lb small white onions, peeled

2 tomatoes, diced

1 small green pepper, diced

1 clove garlic

1 tsp chopped parsley

EQUIPMENT

large skillet   small bowl

PREPARATION

Heat   oil in skillet over moderate heat, and sear meat cubes, turning them to brown evenly.

Combine   flour and paprika, and add to meat, stirring well.

Cook   2 minutes; then add black pepper and bay leaf, and wine if desired.

Simmer   1 hour, covered, on very low heat, or until meat is tender, adding a little hot water from time to time as needed to prevent sticking; then add onions, tomatoes, green pepper, and garlic.

Simmer   covered, until onions are done; then remove bay leaf and garlic.

Serve   hot with parsley as garnish.

CYPRUS   **PORK SIMMERED IN WINE**

SERVINGS: 8
TIME NEEDED: 15 minutes, plus simmering time

INGREDIENTS

3 lbs lean boneless pork,   *1 cup dry red wine*
   trimmed and cut into 1-inch   *¼ tsp salt*
   cubes   *¼ tsp black pepper*
1 tsp coriander seeds

EQUIPMENT

4-qt Dutch oven

PREPARATION

Combine   all ingredients in Dutch oven.
   Heat   to boiling over moderate heat; then lower heat.
 Simmer   30 to 40 minutes, partially covered, over very low heat
        until pork turns golden brown; make sure pork is thor-
        oughly cooked and liquid is gone, forming a slight glaze
        over meat; if liquid evaporates before meat is cooked, add
        a little more wine to finish cooking and to keep meat from
        sticking or scorching.
  Serve   hot.

This dish is traditionally served with fried potatoes, similar to the
American version known as "home fries."

FRANCE

VEAL CHOPS WITH MUSHROOMS

SERVINGS: 4

TIME NEEDED: 15 minutes, plus simmering time

INGREDIENTS

4 lean veal chops, trimmed
½ cup fine bread crumbs
2 Tbs margarine
6 small scallions, finely
  chopped
2 heaping Tbs chopped parsley
10 large fresh tarragon leaves,
  or 2½ tsps dried tarragon

⅛ tsp salt
¼ tsp black pepper
½ lb coarsely chopped
  mushrooms
⅔ cup dry white wine

EQUIPMENT

board or platter   paper towels   large skillet   chopper

PREPARATION

Wipe   veal chops with wet paper towels to moisten surface of meat.

Spread   crumbs on board and dip moistened meat in crumbs, covering both sides well.

Melt   margarine in skillet over moderate heat, and sauté chops, turning to brown both sides; then add scallions, parsley, tarragon, salt, and pepper.

Simmer   10 minutes, covered, on low heat; then add mushrooms and wine.

Simmer   30 minutes, or until meat is tender, turning chops twice to cover evenly with seasonings and sauce.

Serve   hot.

This dish is often served with rice or baked potatoes.

ITALY # BRAISED BEEF

SERVINGS: 4–6

TIME NEEDED: 40 minutes, plus simmering time

INGREDIENTS

1 Tb olive oil	¼ tsp black pepper
1 small onion, chopped	⅛ tsp paprika
2 large garlic cloves, minced	¼ tsp dried oregano
2 lbs lean beef, top or bottom	⅛ tsp dried rosemary
round, trimmed	1 cup dry red wine
⅛ tsp salt	

EQUIPMENT

chopper   4-qt Dutch oven

PREPARATION

Heat   oil in Dutch oven over moderate heat, add onion and garlic, and brown lightly.

Add   beef, salt, pepper, paprika, oregano, and rosemary.

Cook   30 minutes, covered, turning meat occasionally until well browned; then lower heat, and add wine.

Simmer   about 2 hours, or until meat is tender.

ITALY   **LAMB WITH ARTICHOKES**

SERVINGS: 6–8
TIME NEEDED: 45 minutes, plus simmering time

INGREDIENTS

2 Tbs olive oil
1 Tb flour
2½ lbs lean boneless lamb,
  trimmed and cut into 1-inch
  cubes
1 tsp dried sage

½ tsp fennel seeds
⅓ cup wine vinegar*
20 ozs frozen artichokes,
  thawed
juice of 2 large lemons
¼ cup chopped parsley

EQUIPMENT

large skillet or 4-qt Dutch oven   chopper   juicer   slotted spoon

PREPARATION

Heat   oil in skillet over moderate heat.

Dust   flour over meat cubes, add to skillet, and turn cubes to cook evenly until very well browned.

Add   sage and fennel seeds; gradually add wine vinegar, stirring to let liquid evaporate almost completely; then lower heat.

Simmer   45 minutes, covered, stirring occasionally, and adding a little water if necessary to keep meat from sticking; then add artichokes.

Simmer   15 minutes, then add lemon juice and parsley.

Simmer   5 minutes, stirring thoroughly.

Serve   hot, using slotted spoon to remove meat and artichokes.

To use sauce left in pan, skim fat off first, or let it set in refrigerator until fat rises to the top so it can be removed.

*This dish is often made with dry white wine. Substitute 1 cup of wine for wine vinegar, if desired.

LEBANON ## LAMB WITH GREEN BEANS

SERVINGS: 6

TIME NEEDED: 30 minutes, plus simmering time

INGREDIENTS

1 Tb vegetable oil

1 lb lean boneless lamb, trimmed and cut into 1-inch cubes

2 medium onions, chopped

2 large garlic cloves, minced

⅛ tsp ground cinnamon

⅛ tsp salt

¼ tsp black pepper

¾ cup water

2 lbs fresh green beans, cut into 2-inch pieces*

8 ozs canned tomato sauce, or 3 medium fresh tomatoes cut into small pieces

EQUIPMENT

4-qt Dutch oven   small bowl or plate   chopper

PREPARATION

Heat   oil in Dutch oven over moderate heat and add lamb, stirring occasionally until lightly browned all over; then set meat aside in bowl.

Cook   onions and garlic in hot oil until tender; then lower heat, and add cinnamon, salt, and pepper.

Cook   2 minutes, stirring constantly; then add browned meat and ¼ cup water.

Simmer   10 minutes, covered, add green beans, tomato sauce, and ½ cup water.

Simmer   20 to 25 minutes, covered, or until beans are tender.

*Thawed frozen beans, or drained canned beans may be used, but reduce the final simmering time by 10 to 15 minutes.

MAURITANIA   **LAMB BROCHETTES**

YIELD: 6–8 kabobs
TIME NEEDED: 20 minutes, plus marinating and broiling time

INGREDIENTS

½ cup vegetable oil
¾ tsp cayenne pepper
2 lbs lean boneless lamb,
    trimmed and cut into
    1½-inch cubes

16 ozs canned tomato sauce
½ cup water
⅛ tsp salt

EQUIPMENT

2-qt shallow baking dish   1-qt saucepan   skewers

PREPARATION

Combine | oil in baking dish with ½ tsp pepper.
Marinate | meat cubes 2 hours in oil-pepper mixture in the refrigerator or in a cool place, turning occasionally to make sure all pieces come in contact with marinade.
Combine | tomato sauce, water, ¼ tsp pepper, and salt in saucepan.
Heat | to boiling over moderate heat; then lower heat and simmer 5 minutes; turn heat very low to keep sauce warm.
Preheat | broiler or prepare barbecue grill.
Broil | lamb cubes on skewers for 2 to 3 minutes on each side, 4 inches from heat source, or until done to preference.
Serve | hot kabobs with hot, seasoned tomato sauce from baking dish.

ROMANIA

PORK CHOPS WITH
APPLES AND ONIONS

SERVINGS: 6
TIME NEEDED: 30 minutes, plus baking time

INGREDIENTS

2 Tbs vegetable oil
6 lean pork chops, trimmed
2 large garlic cloves, minced
3 medium onions, sliced

3 tart cooking apples, peeled
   and sliced
1/8 tsp salt
1/4 tsp black pepper

EQUIPMENT

4-qt Dutch oven   paper towels   platter

PREPARATION

Preheat oven to 350°F.

Heat oil in Dutch oven over moderate heat; brown chops on both sides; then drain on paper towels on platter and set aside.

Cook garlic and onions in Dutch oven, stirring occasionally until lightly browned; add apple slices, stirring constantly until lightly browned; then remove from heat.

Add salt and pepper, and stir thoroughly.

Place chops on top of apple-onion mixture in Dutch oven.

Bake 1 hour, covered, or until pork is completely tender.

RWANDA   **BEEF STEW WITH VEGETABLES**

SERVINGS: 8
TIME NEEDED: 30 minutes, plus simmering time

INGREDIENTS

2 Tbs vegetable oil
2 lbs beef (shin, or lean-soup or stew beef), cut into 2-inch pieces
2 large onions, sliced
1 large zucchini, cut into 2-inch pieces
½ head cabbage, thickly sliced
1 small cauliflower, separated into florets

1½ lbs potatoes, peeled and halved
1 cup fresh peas
¼ tsp salt
½ tsp black pepper
½ tsp dried sage
2 qts water

EQUIPMENT

peeler   7-qt Dutch oven   paper towels   platter

PREPARATION

Heat   oil in Dutch oven over moderate heat, and brown beef well all over; then set meat aside to drain on paper towels on platter.

Cook   onions in remaining fat, stirring occasionally until lightly browned; add browned meat, plus all remaining ingredients.

Heat   to boiling, then reduce to very low heat.

Simmer   1½ to 2 hours, or until meat is tender, but do *not* let vegetables get completely mushy.

SINGAPORE **MARINATED PORK CHOPS**

SERVINGS: 8

TIME NEEDED: 60 minutes, plus marinating time

INGREDIENTS

¼ cup cornstarch

¼ cup soy sauce, preferably
   low-salt variety

8 lean pork chops, trimmed

6 Tbs flour

2 Tbs vegetable oil

EQUIPMENT

small bowl   large shallow baking pan   large skillet
ovenproof platter

PREPARATION

Combine   cornstarch in bowl with soy sauce; then dip pork chops in sauce, coating well on both sides.

Arrange   chops in single layer in baking pan and marinate in refrigerator for 1 to 2 hours, or longer, until ready to cook; then sprinkle flour over chops, covering both sides.

Preheat   oven to 200°F.

Heat   oil in skillet over moderate heat, or use only enough oil to cover bottom of pan and allow browning of chops.*

Add   as many chops as possible without crowding, and cook 8 to 10 minutes on first side, until crisp and golden brown.

Turn   chops and repeat browning procedure until all are cooked on both sides; keep cooked chops in warm oven until all are done.

Serve   immediately, while hot.

*If you prefer, chops can be baked in a moderate oven until tender.

SYRIA   # LAMB BALLS

SERVINGS: 8
TIME NEEDED: 45 minutes, plus simmering time

INGREDIENTS

2 lbs lean ground lamb   1 tsp oregano
⅓ cup pine nuts   ¼ cup dry bread crumbs
¼ cup golden raisins   1 egg
⅛ tsp salt   ¼ cup flour
1 tsp paprika   2 Tbs vegetable oil
1 tsp turmeric

EQUIPMENT

large bowl   large skillet   paper towels   large platter

PREPARATION

Mix   lamb thoroughly in bowl with all ingredients except flour
         and oil.

Spread   flour on platter.

Shape   meat mixture into small balls, about 1½ inches across, and
         roll each one lightly in flour.

Heat   oil in skillet over moderate heat, cook some meatballs until
         evenly browned all over; then set on platter with paper
         towel to drain fat; repeat procedure until all meatballs are
         browned.

Rewarm   lamb balls in skillet on low heat.

Simmer   15 minutes, covered.

Serve   hot.

Traditionally this is served with a sauce, such as the Eggplant Sauce
on page 225.

UNITED STATES PORK CHOPS WITH SWEET-AND-SOUR SAUCE

SERVINGS: 2

TIME NEEDED: 30 minutes, plus baking time

INGREDIENTS

2 lean thick pork chops,
  trimmed
½ cup sugar
¼ cup white vinegar
¼ cup water
⅛ tsp salt

1 Tb chopped green pepper
1 tsp cornstarch
1 tsp water
½ tsp paprika
1 tsp chopped parsley

EQUIPMENT

1½-qt shallow baking dish   chopper   1-qt saucepan   small dish
or bowl

PREPARATION

Preheat oven to 450°F.

Bake chops 20 to 30 minutes until browned on both sides.

Lower oven to 325°F after meat is browned.

Combine sugar in saucepan with vinegar, ¼ cup water, salt, and green pepper, heat to boiling over high heat; then lower heat and simmer 5 minutes.

Combine cornstarch in small dish with 1 tsp water, stir mixture into hot sauce; then cook until sauce thickens slightly, stirring continuously.

Add paprika and parsley, stirring well, then pour sauce over chops.

Bake 40 minutes, or until meat is tender, occasionally basting with sauce.

VENEZUELA   **SPICY CHOPPED MEAT**

SERVINGS: 4–6

TIME NEEDED: 40–60* minutes, plus simmering time

INGREDIENTS

½ cup raisins

2 Tbs olive oil

½ cup water

⅛ tsp salt

½ tsp black pepper

1 lb lean finely ground beef

½ tsp crushed red pepper

½ tsp tarragon

½ tsp oregano

juice of 1 orange

heaping ¼ tsp freshly grated
  orange rind

2 onions, finely chopped

½ cup chili sauce or ketchup

EQUIPMENT

grater   juicer   chopper   small bowl   10-inch skillet   large fork

PREPARATION

Soak   raisins covered with cold water in bowl.

Heat   oil in skillet over moderate heat, add water, salt, and black pepper, heat to boiling; then lower heat.

Stir   ground beef into mixture, breaking up pieces of meat thoroughly with large fork.

Simmer   5 minutes, covered, stirring occasionally to break up clumps of meat; mix in red pepper, tarragon, oregano, and orange juice.

Simmer   5 minutes, stirring to separate meat into tiny pieces; then add orange rind, onions, drained raisins, and chili sauce.

Simmer   20 minutes, covered, stirring occasionally and adding small amount of water, if needed, to keep mixture from drying out too much.

Serve   hot.

*Depending on whether meat is freshly ground at home, or purchased already ground.

AUSTRIA   **NUT BARS**

YIELD: 12 nut bars
TIME NEEDED: 30 minutes, plus baking time

INGREDIENTS

1–2 tsps margarine
1 cup sugar
1 lb walnuts, finely ground
2 egg whites
½ tsp grated lemon rind

1 tsp lemon juice
granulated sugar for sprinkling
1 egg white
¾ cup confectioners' sugar

EQUIPMENT

grinder or processor   medium bowl   grater   small saucepan
pastry board   small bowl   beater   baking sheet, well greased

PREPARATION

Preheat   oven to 250°F.

Melt   1 tsp margarine in saucepan over very low heat.

Combine   sugar and nuts in medium bowl, add 2 unbeaten egg whites, lemon rind, lemon juice, and melted margarine.

Knead   mixture until it acquires a doughlike consistency and sticks together well enough to be shaped; then place on board sprinkled lightly with granulated sugar, and shape into a rectangle about ½ inch thick and 3 inches wide.

Beat   1 egg white in small bowl until stiff, fold in confectioners' sugar gradually; then cover dough with egg-white topping.

Cut   dough into two long strips, each 1½ inches wide, cut strips into bars about 1 inch wide; then arrange bars on baking sheet.

Bake   20 to 25 minutes; then let cool.

Serve   immediately, or store in airtight container to keep fresh.

CANADA   # GRATED APPLE PIE

SERVINGS: 8
TIME NEEDED: 20 minutes, plus baking time

INGREDIENTS

*1 heaping tsp grated orange
   rind*
1 cup sugar
2 Tbs flour
1 tsp ground cinnamon

½ tsp ground nutmeg
*8 medium tart apples, peeled,
   cored, and coarsely ground*
*unbaked pie shell, single crust**

EQUIPMENT

corer   grater or processor   large bowl   9-inch pie plate

PREPARATION

Preheat   oven to 400°F.
Mix   orange rind, sugar, flour, cinnamon, and nutmeg well, fold-
ing apples in lightly.
Spread   filling into pie shell evenly, smoothing top slightly.
Bake   1 hour, or until crust is light brown and filling begins to
bubble.

*Use a low-salt pie crust, prepared or homemade, such as the Graham-
Cracker Pie Crust on page 112.

LIBERIA ## TAPIOCA CAKE

SERVINGS: 8–12
TIME NEEDED: 20 minutes, plus baking time

INGREDIENTS

1 egg
1¼ cups minute tapioca, or
  raw, grated cassava
½ cup milk
6 Tbs margarine

1 cup sugar
½ cup flour
2½ tsps baking powder
pinch of salt
1 tsp vanilla extract

EQUIPMENT

8-inch, square cake pan, nonstick or lightly greased   small bowl
whisk   medium bowl   sifter

PREPARATION

Preheat   oven to 400°F.
Beat   egg with whisk in small bowl, mix in tapioca plus milk; then set aside 5 minutes.
Cream   margarine in medium bowl with sugar, and blend tapioca batter into margarine-sugar mixture.*
Sift   flour together with baking powder and salt, then add flour mixture and vanilla to batter, stirring well.
Bake   40 minutes, or until tester comes out dry when inserted into center of cake.
Serve   warm, generally with a whipped topping or vanilla ice cream.

*Traditionally ¼ cup shredded or grated coconut is added to margarine-sugar mixture. Coconut is omitted in this recipe because of its relatively high saturated fat content.

NEPAL   **SWEET RICE WITH RAISINS**

SERVINGS: 6–8
TIME NEEDED: 30 minutes, plus standing time

INGREDIENTS

1 cup uncooked long-grain rice	*¼ cup seedless raisins*
1⅓ cups milk	*½ tsp ground cardamom*
⅓ cup sugar	*¼ tsp saffron*
3 Tbs margarine	

EQUIPMENT

medium bowl   strainer   1-qt saucepan   2-qt saucepan

PREPARATION

Cover   rice with cold water in bowl, and set aside 2 hours; then drain thoroughly.

Combine   milk in 1-qt saucepan with sugar, and heat to boiling over moderate heat; then reduce heat to low.

Simmer   5 minutes, stirring to prevent sticking or scorching; then remove from heat.

Melt   margarine in 2-qt saucepan over moderate heat, add drained rice, stirring constantly until rice turns light brown; then add milk-sugar mixture, heat to boiling, and lower heat.

Simmer   15 minutes, covered, and cook rice until softened but still somewhat firm and crunchy; do *not* let rice get mushy; then add remaining ingredients.*

Cook   5 minutes, blending well.

Add a very small amount of milk from time to time, if needed, to keep rice from clumping and drying out before the final step.

*Traditionally 2 Tbs shredded coconut are added at this step. However, coconut may be omitted because of its relatively high saturated fat content.

THE NETHERLANDS **RHINE WINE
WHIP**

SERVINGS: 6–8
TIME NEEDED: 45 minutes, plus chilling time

INGREDIENTS

4 eggs   juice of 2 lemons
½ cup sugar   ½ cup dry Rhine wine
1 Tb grated lemon rind

EQUIPMENT

grater   juicer   large bowl   double boiler   whisk   electric mixer
large serving bowl or individual dessert dishes

PREPARATION

Heat   water in bottom of double boiler over moderate heat;
            then lower heat until water simmers.

Separate egg whites to bowl.

Combine   egg yolks in top of double boiler (remove from heat) with
            sugar, lemon rind, and lemon juice; then beat with whisk
            until smooth.

Add   wine gradually, blending well; then cook egg mixture
            over simmering water, stirring constantly until mixture
            thickens.

Beat   egg whites with electric beater until very stiff peaks form;
            then beat gently with whisk into yolk mixture, a little at
            a time, over simmering water, until the whip becomes
            light and fluffy.

Pour   into serving bowl or individual dishes to cool.

Chill   2 to 3 hours in refrigerator after whip has cooled.

RUSSIA   # FRUIT DIAMONDS

SERVINGS: 12 (two small diamonds per person)
TIME NEEDED: 25 minutes, plus baking time

INGREDIENTS

margarine for greasing pan
1 cup blanched almonds,
    chopped
1 cup walnuts, chopped
1 cup dried apricots, chopped
1 cup dried currants

1 cup raisins
1 cup thick raspberry or
    strawberry jam
2 eggs*
1 tsp vanilla extract
2 cups flour, sifted

EQUIPMENT

shallow 11 × 15-inch baking pan   chopper   medium bowl   sifter
sharp slicing knife   cooling rack

PREPARATION

Preheat   oven to 300°F.
   Coat   baking pan lightly with margarine.
  Blend   almonds, walnuts, and apricots in bowl thoroughly with all
          remaining ingredients except flour.
Sprinkle flour over batter and mix thoroughly; pour into baking pan.
   Bake   35 minutes.
 Remove   pan and cut baked fruit into diamond shapes by cutting
          diagonally, first in one direction, then in opposite direction.
   Bake   5 minutes more to dry out cut edges of diamonds.
   Cool   on cake rack.

*To lower cholesterol content, only use one egg plus two egg whites.

TURKEY ## YOGURT PASTRY

SERVINGS: 12

TIME NEEDED: 45 minutes, plus baking time

INGREDIENTS

2 cups sugar
2½ cups water
1 tsp lemon juice
3 eggs
1 cup sugar
1 cup flour

1 tsp baking powder
¼ tsp salt
1 heaping tsp grated lemon rind
1 cup yogurt

EQUIPMENT

square 9 × 9-inch baking pan, nonstick or lightly greased
2-qt saucepan   large mixing bowl   whisk or beater   grater
sifter   sharp slicing knife

PREPARATION

Preheat oven to 375°F.

Stir 2 cups sugar, water, and lemon juice in saucepan over moderate heat, cook until sugar dissolves completely, stirring occasionally; let boil 20 minutes until mixture becomes syrupy, then remove syrup from heat and cool.

Mix eggs in bowl with 1 cup sugar, and beat until thick.

Sift flour, baking powder, and salt; then combine half the flour mixture with eggs and grated lemon rind; add yogurt, mixing well, and add remainder of flour mixture, blending thoroughly.

Bake 20 to 30 minutes in baking pan until top is lightly browned, or until cake tester comes out clean when inserted into middle of cake.

Cut slightly cooled cake diagonally across at 2-inch intervals in one direction, repeating same cuts in opposite direction for diamond-shaped portions, each about 2 inches across; then immediately pour cooled syrup over cake.

Let cake stand until cool and syrup has been absorbed.

Chill thoroughly in refrigerator before serving plain, or with whipped topping.

UNITED STATES   HOT PRUNE FLUFF

SERVINGS: 8–10
TIME NEEDED: 30 minutes, plus baking time

INGREDIENTS

margarine for greasing soufflé
  dish
1 tsp + ⅓ cup granulated
  sugar
¾ cup very finely chopped
  pitted prunes

6 egg whites
1 Tb confectioners' sugar
¼ cup pulverized pecans
whipped topping

EQUIPMENT

chopper or processor   medium bowl   large bowl   beater
8–10-cup casserole or soufflé dish   shallow baking pan

PREPARATION

Preheat oven to 350°F.
  Grease soufflé dish lightly with margarine, and sprinkle 1 tsp sugar
         lightly over the inside.
    Mix ⅓ cup sugar into prunes.*
   Beat egg whites until stiff peaks form; then fold sweetened
         prunes lightly into egg whites, and spoon mixture into
         soufflé dish.
    Set soufflé dish into baking pan filled with 1–2 inches water.
   Bake 40 minutes.
Sprinkle confectioners' sugar and pecans on top of baked prune
         fluff; then add whipped topping.
  Serve hot.

Traditionally, this recipe calls for a sweet whipped cream topping,
but if that is contrary to your diet, a whipped topping can be used
such as the one on page 199.

*If prunes are tart, use ½–¾ cup sugar.

UNITED STATES   ## MERINGUE CUPS

SERVINGS: 8–12
TIME NEEDED: 30 minutes, plus baking time

INGREDIENTS

4 egg whites	*1 tsp cream of tartar*
¼ tsp salt	*1 cup sugar*

EQUIPMENT

baking sheet   heavy freezer-type paper, ungreased   whisk or
beater   large bowl   cup of warm water   round soup spoon,
measuring spoon of same size, or teaspoon

PREPARATION

Preheat oven to 250°F.

Cover baking sheet with layer of ungreased paper.

Beat egg whites until very foamy; then add salt, beating well,
plus cream of tartar, continuing to beat well.

Add sugar, but *only 1 Tb at a time,* continuing to beat well as
each spoonful is added until very stiff peaks form.

Scoop 1 spoonful of meringue onto paper on baking sheet.

Dip spoon into warm water and press back of spoon down into
center of meringue to form a hollow or "cup."

Repeat procedure until all meringue is shaped into "cups."

Bake 60 minutes, or until meringue is dry and "brittle."

Cool before serving with filling of fresh berries, fruit, sherbet, or
ice cream.

For medium-large meringue cups to serve 8, scoop larger amounts
onto baking sheet and use soup spoon to make "cups." For serving 12,
scoop smaller amounts of meringue onto baking sheet and use back
of teaspoon to form "cups."

UNITED STATES   **MRS. TRUMAN'S
OZARK PUDDING**

SERVINGS: 4–5
TIME NEEDED: 25 minutes, plus baking time

INGREDIENTS

1 egg	1¼ tsps baking powder
¾ cup sugar	½ cup chopped apples
2 Tbs flour	½ cup chopped pecans

EQUIPMENT

8-inch pie plate, greased or nonstick   chopper   beater
medium mixing bowl

PREPARATION

Preheat   oven to 350°F.
Beat   egg very thoroughly; then add sugar and beat until creamy.
Sift   flour with baking powder.
Add   flour to egg mixture and beat until well blended.
Fold   apples and pecans into batter.
Pour   well-mixed batter into pie plate.
Bake   35 minutes or until firm and golden brown.*
Serve   hot, warm, or cold.

*Do not be alarmed if pudding rises high during baking, then falls before it is removed from the oven. This is supposed to happen.

REFERENCES

Blankenhorn, D. H., et al. "The Influence of Diet on the Appearance of New Lesions in Human Coronary Arteries," *Journal of the American Medical Association* 263, no. 12 (March 1990), 1646.

Council on Scientific Affairs, American Medical Association. "Dietary Fiber and Health," *Journal of the American Medical Association* 262, no. 4 (July 28, 1989), 542.

Esterbauer, H. "The Role of Vitamin E and Carotenoids in Preventing the Oxidation of Low Density Lipoprotein," presented at the New York Academy of Sciences conference on Vitamin E: Biochemistry and Health Implications, November 1988.

Fuchart, J. C., et al. "Antioxidant Therapy and Uptake of Human Oxidized LDL by Macrophages," *SERLIA,* Institute Pasteur, Lille, France, 1988.

Hays, A. H., Jr. "Advances in Cardiovascular Pharmacology," *Journal of the American Medical Association* 248, no. 5 (August 6, 1982), 537.

Kraus, B. *The Barbara Kraus Cholesterol Counter.* New York: Perigee Books, 1985.

————. *Barbara Kraus Complete Guide to Sodium.* New York: New American Library, 1990.

————. *The Barbara Kraus 30-Day Cholesterol Program.* New York: Perigee Books, 1988.

Sempos, C., et al. "The Prevalence of High Blood Cholesterol Levels Among Adults in the United States," *Journal of the American Medical Association* 262, no. 1 (July 7, 1989), 45.

Story, J. A. "Nutrition Cure-All Doesn't Replace Balanced Diet," Purdue University Press Release (March 27, 1989), presented at the American Chemical Society meeting, Dallas, April 10, 1989.

INDEX (GENERAL)

INDEX BY COUNTRY/REGION OF RECIPE ORIGIN

ABOUT THE AUTHORS

Barbara Kraus, noted cook and food authority, won instant acclaim with her bestseller *Calories and Carbohydrates,* and her pioneering work *The Dictionary of Sodium, Fats, and Cholesterol.* She is credited with helping arouse public consciousness of the importance of eating both well and wisely. Her master's degree in anthropology focused largely on the cultural aspects of food uses and cooking habits. Her many works include the popular cookbooks *The Cookbook of the United Nations* and *The Cookbook to Serve 2, 6, or 24.*

Margaret Markham is a veteran medical writer and coauthor of *The Breast Book.* Her articles have appeared in leading national publications including *Redbook, Harper's Bazaar, Parents Magazine,* and *Encyclopaedia Britannica.* Formerly editor of *American Baby Magazine* and executive director of the Vitamin Information Bureau, she has long championed the importance of good nutrition at all ages.

Ordering is easy and convenient. Just call 1-800-631-8571 or send your order to:

The Putnam Publishing Group
390 Murray Hill Parkway, Dept. B
East Rutherford, NJ 07073

Also available at your local bookstore or wherever paperbacks are sold.

		PRICE	
		U.S.	CANADA
The Barbara Kraus 30-Day Cholesterol Program	399-51508	$ 6.95	$ 9.25
The Dictionary of Sodium, Fats, and Cholesterol	399-51572	12.95	16.95
The Barbara Kraus Cholesterol Counter	399-51134	6.95	9.25
The Barbara Kraus Calorie Counter	399-51222	6.95	9.25
The Columbia Encyclopedia of Nutrition	399-51573	12.95	16.95
Carlton Frederick's New Low Blood Sugar and You	399-51087	7.95	10.50
Hold the Fat, Sugar & Salt	399-51073	7.95	10.50
Dr. Bruce Lowell's Fat % Finder	399-51653	8.95	11.75
The Barbara Kraus International Cookbook	399-51655	14.95	19.50

Subtotal $ _____

*Postage & handling: $1.00 for 1 book, 25¢ for each additional book up to a maximum of $3.50

*Postage & handling $ _____

Sales Tax $ _____
(CA, NJ, NY, PA)

Total Amount Due $ _____
Payable in U.S. Funds
(No cash orders accepted)

Please send me the titles I've checked above.
Enclosed is my ☐ check   ☐ money order
Please charge my ☐ Visa   ☐ MasterCard   ☐ American Express
Card # _____   Expiration date _____
Signature as on charge card _____
Name _____
Address _____
City _____ State _____ Zip _____

Please allow six weeks for delivery. Prices subject to change without notice.